CAGOLL

Se

Pearl

This new two-hour play for r
commissioned by the BBC an

CW00967923

'John Arden's *Pearl* poured into the ear a two-hour tumult of character, action and ideas, infused with irony, enriched with intellect, performed with passion . . .

Pearl is a mysterious lady with a strange accent . . . The time is the late 1630's, the political and religious climate is deeply troubled, the moment could be right for something extraordinary to happen which will change the course of history. The means of change, we learn, may be through the theatre and in particular through the performance of a play, partly to be written by Pearl . . .

That the argument takes such strange root in the mind is due to Arden's vivid and peotic gift. He keeps unlocking doors between history and possibility.' Gillian Reynolds, *Daily Telegraph.*

Despite its historical setting, the play has a deal of relevance to modern Britain — and to modern Ireland. In his preface the author concludes that 'maybe there is still good reason for re-examining an earlier period of history when disastrous decisions were taken for the most plausible motives, when everyone was aware that the times were highly critical, and yet so few could divest themselves of their erroneous received ideas.

Pearl was nominated for a Giles Cooper Award as one of the best radio plays of 1978.

The photograph on the front cover shows Elizabeth Bell as Pearl and David Calder as Tom Backhouse recording the play for the BBC broadcast. London Weekend Television Copyright Photograph by Simon Farrell. The photograph of John Arden on the back cover is a Radio Times Copyright Photograph by Peter Howe.

Also in Methuen's Modern Plays

Plays by John Arden

SERJEANT MUSGRAVE'S DANCE
THE WORKHOUSE DONKEY
IRONHAND
(adapted from Goethe's
Goetz von Berlichingen)
ARMSTRONG'S LAST GOODNIGHT

Plays by John Arden and Margaretta D'Arcy

THE BUSINESS OF GOOD GOVERNMENT
THE ROYAL PARDON
THE HERO RISES UP
THE ISLAND OF THE MIGHTY

In the Master Playwrights Series

ARDEN PLAYS: ONE
*(Serjeant Musgrave's Dance,
Armstrong's Last Goodnight,
The Workhouse Donkey)*

Also by John Arden

TO PRESENT THE PRETENCE
Essays on the Theatre and its Public

Also available from Eyre Metheun

BEST RADIO PLAYS OF 1978
*The Giles Cooper Award Winners
(published in association with the BBC)*

Pearl

A PLAY ABOUT A PLAY WITHIN THE PLAY

Written for radio by

John Arden

EYRE METHUEN
LONDON

First published 1979 by Eyre Methuen Ltd
11 New Fetter Lane, London EC4P 4EE

© 1979 by John Arden
Printed in Great Britain by
Cox & Wyman Ltd, Fakenham, Norfolk

ISBN 0 413 40090 5 (Hardback)
ISBN 0 413 40100 6 (Paperback)

Author's Note

The story of *Pearl* takes place in England some time around 1640.

I am vague about the date because the history is distorted in the play for the convenience and simplification of the plot: but not, I hope, so far as to falsify it altogether. I have, for instance, deliberately forgotten about the Short Parliament that preceded the Long Parliament; and I have not troubled to find any evidence that Irish rebels were transported to the American colonies as early as the reign of James I — though they certainly were later. If Owen Roe O'Neill in fact tried to gain the support of the Parliamentary Party in England before the Irish Rising of 1641, he was not successful, and historians today do not appear to know about it. He did make an attempt at something of the sort, via the professionally non-political military politician Monck, after Charles I had been defeated and executed. It was then too late: and Parliament refused to allow Monck to continue negotiations. Cromwell, at this time, was already on the way to Ireland. The results of his notorious expedition are still brought to mind every day by the news from Belfast and points north. Similarly, I have no knowledge of any writer who made a serious endeavour to present republican ideals upon the professional stage at this period. If it had been possible, say, for John Bunyan to have written plays and had them produced, our theatre would have found for itself a very different history. By Bunyan's time it was not only too late: it was ideologically inconceivable. Yet Bunyan's genius was of a very similar nature to that of the authors of the late-mediaeval morality plays: a true theatrical instinct runs through every line of *The Pilgrim's Progress*.

All the characters whose voices are heard in the play are inventions of my own. The O'Neills, of course, the King, the Lord Deputy (Strafford), and some other persons referred to in the dialogue are historical.

There is something finally futile, I suppose, about plays that are written from the premise: 'If only it had happened otherwise . . .' But so long as our writers today (purportedly the collective voice of enlightened British cultural values — or if they aren't, who is?) remain unable to decide whether negotiations over royalties with the state-supported National Theatre, for example, should take priority, as an immediate issue for agitation, over state-supporting torture in the Ulster police-stations: so long as our Trade Union movement refuses to recognise the reality of seventeenth-century colonialist sectarianism within its own ranks, aborting any honest view of the unjustifiable 'British presence' in the North of Ireland: so long as the General Staff of the British Army is allowed to play its professionally non-political games of politics around the so-called *security* of those Six Counties: and so long as all proper progress in such affairs is muffled and diverted by cooked-up fears of a putative 'blood-bath' — then maybe there is still good reason for re-examining an earlier period of history when disastrous decisions were taken for the most plausible motives, when everyone was aware that the times were highly critical, and yet so few could divest themselves of their erroneous received ideas.

The play, as presented on the BBC, fitted neatly into a two-hour slot. This text is rather longer. The cuts made for the broadcast are indicated in square brackets. Two scenes (Five and Nine) have abridged versions provided in the appendices.

John Arden
Galway and London 1977-8

DRAMATIS PERSONAE *(main voices only):*

PEARL   a Messenger, from the west, of no recognizable speech nor nation, she invents her own shape as she goes, and has earned money from it upon public stages. Hard to tell by what cause she will be moved to passion, or will choose to move others: but certain she will be sudden at it. Between twenty and thirty years old.

BACKHOUSE   comes from Yorkshire, writes plays, has been perhaps disappointed in love as a young man: but his hair is now gray and his spirit more truculent than it used to be. Regards himself as the best in his line since Aristophanes: but would be astonished if anyone were to share his opinion.

Lord GRIMSCAR   a great Nobleman, conscientious for the public good: aware that his own good is not always believed by others to be synonymous. Regrets this circumstance, but has hopes that one day the world will discover its error. His understanding of his own good is susceptible, however, to persuasion from many quarters. Aged forty.

BELLADONNA   a widowed Countess, rich, libidinous, large, political: and in the upshot vindictive. Said to have been painted naked by Rubens, in character as 'Angelica, with a Hermit'. Thirty-five years old.

The DUCHESS   Belladonna's cousin, her exemplar and instructress in all things public and private, much relied on by great men for her intuitive statecraft. Aged sixty.

GIDEON GRIP   a Puritan preacher: of great sincerity and power. No ranter. His apocalyptic jargon is a tool of his trade, as a chisel or plane for his other trade, carpentry.

BARNABAS   the best Actor in England.

Doctor SOWSE   a time-serving Clergyman, slave to his base vices, a good reason for Gideon Grip.

Captain CATSO   a Mercenary. Seeking employment upon cruel work, he must boast his own cruelty and deceit even beyond the reality, which is none the less disgusting.

KATERINA   an Actress. As this is an unprecedented profession in England, she brings to it the technique of her original calling in the stews.

Mother BUMROLL   Bawd and Pawnbroker: soft-hearted and hard-headed, makes a profit both ways.

Pearl was first broadcast on BBC Radio 4 on 3 July 1978.
The cast was as follows:

PEARL	Elizabeth Bell
MOTHER BUMROLL	Paula Tilbrook
BARNABAS/MALE VOICE	David Mahlowe
STAGE MANAGER/	
CASCA/ACTOR	John Jardine
GRIP	Geoffrey Banks
SOWSE/CAESAR	Ronald Herdman
GRIMSCAR/1st COMMONER	Peter Jeffrey
BACKHOUSE/	
SOOTHSAYER	David Calder
BELLADONNA	Lynda Marchal
DUCHESS	Kathleen Helme
CATSO/MARULLUS	Kenneth Alan Taylor
KATERINA/	
FEMALE VOICE	Jane Knowles
MESSENGER/	
FLAVIUS/ACTOR	Robert Morton

Music specially composed and directed by Stephen Boxer
Musicians Ephraim Segerman and members of the Northern Renaissance Consort

Produced by Alfred Bradley

Scene One

*Actors performing 'Julius Caesar' in an echoing hall. After a
flourish of music, they start at Act One, Scene One. There is a
sprinkling of applause as the beginners march out with heavy
footsteps onto the stage. The audience makes occasional muttered
conversation, not loudly enough to be understood, but conveying
a general sense of lack of interest in the play. Feet are shuffled,
benches creak etc. The style of presentation of the Shakespearian
dialogue is old-fashioned, but in no sense parodied — strongly
declamatory and rhetorical. We hear it as though from the back
of the hall.*

ACTOR *(playing Flavius).*
   'Hence! Home, you idle creatures, get you home:
   Is this a holiday? What! Know you not,
   Being mechanical you ought not walk
   Upon a labouring day, without the sign
   Of your profession? Speak, what trade art thou?'
ACTOR *(playing 1st Commoner).*
   'Why, sir, a carpenter.'
ACTOR *(playing Marullus).*
   'Where is thy leather apron and thy rule?
   What dost thou with thy best apparel on . . .?'

> *The Actors' voices fade down slightly but continue the scene
> as a background for the ensuing dialogue.*

PEARL *(to herself).* So this then is the King's England: all my life
   I have heard them talk of it, and here for the first time I sit.
   You might say, in the middle of England, the mere English
   packed solid like a shop-board of pork-pies gazing up at the
   gaudy platform at what else but themselves, self-glorified in
   the role of Rome. Do they like what they are looking at? I am

so curious to see their faces that I have scarce had time to take
note of what's happening so far upon the stage: but it is surely
more vehement than any reflection I can detect back here
among these rain-soaked homespun jackets and these broad-
brimmed black hats. And for myself, in this velvet mask and
the clothes I am wearing — or rather not so much wearing as
gathering them uncertainly around me with both hands —
they have taken one look at me and turned their backs like
a herd of bullocks seeking shelter from the north wind . . .
Oh God, here she comes at me, couldn't she leave me alone one
moment to forget myself one moment in a real loud tragic play . . .?

MOTHER BUMROLL (*her nagging overlaps a little with Pearl's
last sentence*). Here, here, what're you playing at —? Pearl you
daft article, will you uncover them paps at once, take your
shawl off of your shoulders, didn't I tell you you wor put here
in front o't' rest o't girls, on special purpose to attract the
Parson? There he is, look at him there, sat next to t'Mayor and
Aldermen on that bench right up agen stage! I wor told by
them as fetched you here they gave you credit for some good
sense.

PEARL (*in a furious whisper*). I assure you I am not here for my
own pleasure, old woman. I have never done this in this
country before: I have never even been in this country before.
If there is a difference whatever from Toledo or Verona or
Palermo in what you do, I rely upon you to inform me. The
Parson is watching the play at this moment: but as it happens
he has already taken note of me, through the opening of my
shawl, over ten minutes ago, and he grinned at me like a lizard.
Nobody else did: and I am nervous. I tell you I am nervous. It
is clear that in this place they loathe and abominate the very
notion of a courtesan: and I ought to have been forewarned.

MOTHER BUMROLL. God we all ought to have been forewarned.
We've not had a play in this town-hall for nigh on twelve
months, and when we did use to, it wor never *this* crowd came
in to it. I can't think what they're here for. They're not
enjoying it, that's certain.

PEARL. Well I *am*, and I'd be grateful if you'd leave me to let me
do it.

MOTHER BUMROLL. Now now now, lovey, Mother Bumroll does her best . . .

Her voice drifts away.

Alice, where are you, Alice, come out of the back of the alcove and stop eating them bloody sweet-meats. There's a cattle-drover at the far side has his eye upon you, my lass, so do your business, give him a wink and a wave, that's right . . . eh dear, the trade's collapsing wi' the wickedness of these times . . .

PEARL *(to herself)*. They have no women in their plays, they tell me. I wonder is that good or bad. Such actresses as I have known, as I have *been* indeed, actresses . . . little different from the very prostitutes among whom I am now huddled, were we memorable upon the stage for anything else but the hot smell of temptation? While even in sensual Venice they told me there is no sight more remarkable than a comprehensive English tragedy, performed to the trumpet and kettledrum, by a band of men you can respect from the pit of your gut for the power and the discipline and the conviction of their craftsmanship . . .

Cross fade.

Scene Two

The Actors' lines continue direct through, but we are now backstage, and the quality of the sound is muffled.

BARNABAS. Stage-Manager!

STAGE-MANAGER. Mr Barnabas?

BARNABAS. Your impression of the sentiment of the audience, Stage-Manager: not quite usual?

STAGE-MANAGER. We were twenty minutes late in starting, Mr Barnabas, on account of having to wait for Lord Grimscar to arrive, so I'd have expected them restive: but they were downright begrudging before we'd even begun.

BARNABAS. I only hope that my lord knows what he is doing.

Had he not recommended it, I would never have sought this
booking. I have always maintained it is professional suicide to
stick your nose beyond the Pennines. But this is his town, and
he is our patron, and we must do what we are asked to do . . .

ACTOR (*playing Flavius; on stage, coming near as he prepares to
make his exit.*)
'. . . These growing feathers plucked from Caesar's wing
Will make him fly an ordinary pitch,
Who else would soar above the view of men
And keep us all in servile fearfulness.'

STAGE-MANAGER (*during above Actor's speech*). Watch it, Mr
Barnabas, it's your first entrance coming up. Everybody ready
for the entrance of the Procession. *At* the left-hand door, if
you please. Julius Caesar, Calpurnia, Mark Antony and
Senators: Brutus and Cassius at the rear: cue the trumpeter:
One two three and you're on!

Cross fade.

Scene Three

*The actors march out onto the stage, as the trumpet plays a
prolonged flourish, leading into a march-tune from all the
theatre-music. We are again at the back of the audience. The
procession moves right down and round the stage and the music
continues for a good while as the formal tableau of the grand-
entrance is being established.*

PEARL (*to herself, during the music*). Aha, so now we have it . . .!
Spiked gilded diadems, breastplates of pasteboard, chains,
belts, epaulettes, tinselled and sequinned, high orange wigs
above chalk-white Roman faces, looped purple cloaks in thick
folds flying, silk scarves of cramoisie, and a whole regiment of
broad feet in their studded red boots clanging and ringing as
they thunder across the platform . . .

ACTOR (*playing Caesar*). 'Calpurnia!'

ACTOR (*playing Casca*). 'Peace ho! Caesar speaks!'

Music ceases. The Actors' footfalls on the stage sound suddenly very loud — the audience has now gone dead silent.

ACTOR *(playing Caesar)*. 'Calpurnia!'

ACTOR *(playing Calpurnia (a boy))*. 'Here, my lord.'

ACTOR *(playing Caesar)*.
'Stand you directly in Antonius' way
When he doth run his course. Antonius!'

BARNABAS *(playing Mark Antony)*. 'Caesar my lord . . .'

PEARL *(to herself, as the dialogue of Julius Caesar continues)*.
Look at that one now, Mark Antony, the huge captain of the
great emperor, do anything for his huge master, eat, drink,
fornicate, kill . . . God love him, how he loves himself . . .

ACTOR *(playing Caesar)*.
'Forget not in your speed, Antonius,
To touch Calpurnia; for our elders say
The barren, touchéd in this holy chase
Shake off their sterile curse.'

BARNABAS *(playing Mark Antony)*.
'I shall remember,
When Caesar says "Do this": it is performed.'

ACTOR *(playing Caesar)*. 'Set on: and leave no ceremony out.'

The music strikes up the march-tune once more and the Actors' feet resound.

ACTOR *(playing Soothsayer)*. 'Caesar!'

Music stops (we assume a cut here in Mr Barnabas' acting text).

'Beware the Ides of March!'

GRIP *(from the audience, interrupting)*. Beware the Wrath of God!

Sensation.

PEARL *(to herself)*. Wait a minute now, that's no Roman —

GRIP. Beware the Wrath of God!

Catcalls and abusive cries, attempts at 'Shush', shifting and moving of feet and benches, calls of 'Let him speak' etc. The Actors have tried to continue but are unable.

PEARL (*to herself*). — but an old bent threadbare Englishman like a crabapple with wire spectacles, stumbling his big feet as he surges forward over the benches —

GRIP. This mendacious false testimony by persons upon a stage to be other than God made them is obnoxious to the integrity of the Children of God! Would you mind out of my road, Alderman, I am desired to be lifted up, I have the Burden of the Word to deliver unto this assembly, to these easy deluded sheep who will even hear without protest a rogue-and-vagabond of the name of Barnabas proclaim himself Mark Antony. But indeed little of that, the stalwart impudence of such an one is so manifestly throttled by the insidious hermaphrodite bramble-bush that extends itself alongside of him —

PEARL (*to herself*). He must mean that round-eyed boy parading his false bosom under the title of Calpurnia . . . Sure in comparison with a true female player he has the elegance of a pair of compasses: but they cannot want him to go to hell for it . . .?

> *More confusion of shouts, the catcalls are now far less evident than the noises of approval, applause and cries of* 'Hallelujah!'

GRIP. In the name of the decency of Christian human truth, I call upon the godly, upon the remnant of saints in Israel, to associate their voices with my incontinent denunciation!

> *Mounting volume of* 'Hallelujah!'

PEARL (*to herself*). At least a third of 'em, maybe two-thirds. And moreover from all parts of the house. I've a notion this is nothing but a carefully put-up job . . . If it is, I must look clearly to my own proper safety . . . Hold on now, that cheese-faced clergyman's attempting to make himself heard.

SOWSE (*silencing the din, at length*). My prerogative, my prerogative, archiepiscopally preferred here in accordance with the Articles of the Established Church of England, my prerogative will not suffer to be displaced thus *coram populo* upon matters of divinity! Gideon Grip, I know you, you are no

preacher, you are no licensed lecturer, but a profane
blaspheming artisan, a carpenter, Gideon Grip —

GRIP. As was Our Saviour at His trade in Nazareth, Dr Sowse,
and furthermore as was one personage in the first scene of
this play who was set up there on t'stage to be made mock of
and provoked promiscuous! Don't think because we came
here to denounce these works of Satan that we paid no
attention to what was going on inside o'them —

SOWSE. You should attend, sir, to your table-legs, and leave
other folk in peace to their legitimate artistic pastime: as
provided for by the munificence of my lord in the gallery
there, whose gracious presence you insult with your uneducated
canting. Stand down, Gideon Grip, and permit the players to
proceed!

GRIP. I will not! Your Established Church is a stink from the
Devil's fundament —

Strong reactions, pro and con.

GRIMSCAR *(speaks as from an upper level)*. Mr Grip —

GRIP *(ignoring him)*. My lord's presence a foul carbuncle covered
with his ermine robe!

More reactions and some laughter.

(Raising his voice to top them.) Behold Lucifer in his turpitude
on the high tower-tops of Babylon: and who shall stand against
him but a simple tradesman of this Parish wi' nowt but
Scripture within his fist!

Great chorus of 'Hallelujah!'

GRIMSCAR *(endeavours again to get in a word. Now he takes
firm advantage of the moment of silence that follows the
shouts)*. Mr Grip!

More 'Shushing' *and hisses of* 'It's my lord, Lord Grimscar!'
etc.

Mr Grip, would you pause one moment, for breath, if for
nothing else?

More laughter.

GRIMSCAR. Thank you. Will everybody please take note I am not wearing an ermine robe . . .?

PEARL *(to herself, as there is more laughter)*. Indeed he's not — he's in sub-fusc and plain starched linen, and he sits up there amongst his people just as though he were one of their own, you could surely mistake him for a non-too-prosperous haberdasher . . .

GRIMSCAR. And although it is true that the actors have come to entertain us this afternoon at my express invitation, I brought them with but small hope, sir, of relaxing your morality — and most certainly with no hope of subverting the trenchant sermons you deliver every Sabbath in your illegal Conventicle.

SOWSE. Illegal Conventicle — the very words of my lord, my lord makes quite clear that this man Grip is a Sectarian, I cannot understand why the Magistrates have not —

GRIMSCAR. *I* do not propose to go chasing an old carpenter over hedgerow and ditch on the off-chance I might catch him communicating with his Redeemer in terms not approved by Act of Parliament, Dr Sowse —

FEMALE VOICE *(interrupting)*. Parliament — we've got no Parliament — it's been bloody well got rid of at the pleasure of the King!

GRIMSCAR *(ignoring this and the applause that follows)*. Of course, Dr Sowse, if you feel that he should be chased by somebody —

MALE VOICE *(interrupting)*. If somebody reckons to chase him, then there's somebody looking-out to get his neck broke, that's what!

More applause.

GRIMSCAR. That'll do. There's no need here for any threats of bodily violence. Very well. The play is over: 'The True History of Julius Caesar'. I had hoped it might teach some of us that the worst despot in the world is yet vulnerable to the aroused outrage of honest men who love their country. I offer my apologies to Mr Barnabas and his excellent good fellows for the humiliation they have received. Had you listened to them a

little further, I think they would have been able, in the course
of the plot, to justify to everyone their temerity, and mine, in
presenting the play in this town hall. Is that not so, Mr Barnabas?

BARNABAS (*from the stage*). My lord, you have hit it right. We
are justified in nothing but our performance before an audience,
and from that we have been inhibited. We request your
permission gracefully to retire.

GRIMSCAR. Thank you, Mr Barnabas, most dignified indeed: I
have never heard a public reproach administered with more
style. All those who are of my mind will please show their
appreciation.

He leads a moderate demonstration of applause.

Well: there it was: it was a great play, forty years old and
exceeding well-seasoned: but no, you would not hear it. And
so alas, it can not be heard.

Sound of general dispersal begins during the next speech.

BACKHOUSE (*from the audience*). My lord, d'you think *I* might
be heard, for one minute?

GRIMSCAR. Why not, if Mr Grip and the Sons of the Prophets
will extend to you the courtesy? Stand up, Tom, and let them
look at you. Gentlemen, please don't leave! This gentleman is
Tom Backhouse, my present guest at Grimscar Hall. Have you
heard of him? He writes plays and he knows his business. By
God, Tom, I will have *them* know the art of Roscius is more
than pastime. They have described my good friend Barnabas
and all his company as barefaced perjurers: prove them wrong.

GRIP. We are nowt if not amenable to a reasoned disputation —

MALE VOICE. Let's afford him a fair hearing while he justifies
his blasphemy —

FEMALE VOICE. If he can!

GRIP. But he won't!

BACKHOUSE. Whatever you say . . . Mr Mayor, ladies and
gentlemen: to open my argument, let me first of all postulate
that the craft or mystery of an enactment, upon a stage, of a
poet's fable, intendeth not, as is alleged, fraudulently to deceive:
rather do the players endeavour a prior collusion with their

auditory, that these things shall be said and done in frank and
open pretence, assumed acceptable upon both sides.*

From this point in his speech, PEARL's *subsequent speech
is brought up over it.*

(Slowly and drearily.) [Such and such is to be the fable, and all
shall know beforehand that indeed it is but feigned: this and
that are to be the presented personations, achieved by the due
decorum of gesture, speech, prepared garments, prepared paint
upon the face, prepared hair upon the head — what else can
they be but temporary?] Thus a young lad in female clothing
is immediately recognised as being no more than what he is,
an ephemeral poetic emblem for the Generation of Eve,
whereby all natural passion that one half of mankind shall feel
toward the other —

PEARL *(starting at * above).* There's no doubt about it, this Lord
Marquess of Grimscar, whatever his dealings, has a good wit to
contain trouble. [Such a meagre pale fellow to be thought of
as a great lord, yet out of his very pocket, as it were, he can
bring forth peace-and-quiet, and the dullest tame poet that I
ever heard of in the world. But sure, then, why wouldn't he?
Isn't this altogether what they call the true style of England?
A rebellious raving carpenter girded with the bludgeon of the
vengeance of God — and yet within two minutes the same man
will sit down and purse his lips and nod his head, and put his
hand up to his ear for a long-drawn controlled argument — for
a lecture, would you believe?] Can it really be true, what I was
told [before I came here] that this land was about to split with
the full fury of Civil War!

GRIP *has interrupted* BACKHOUSE *with an* 'Ah-ah-ah!'

PEARL. Wait a minute now, there's an objection — your dried-up
brown dog's muzzle of a poet said something he shouldn't . . .?
GRIP. Hold up there! Natural passion? A young lad in female
raiment, you have the nerve to call it natural?
BACKHOUSE. I said, sir, a poetic emblem.
GRIP. Oh aye and an emblem for what? Carnal dealings outside
of wedlock! [And don't you go telling me about frank and

open pretence. By the very splendour of the pretence are such
imaginings put to work. And from the imaginings what else will
men do then but seek at once the reality? As I at this moment,
thus peering and prying, observe nudity and concealment
together, within alcoves, black velvet masks, white skin
bedaubed with paint — and] you'd have me believe this
damned bawdy-house is nowt other than a shrine to the Muses!
I say, pull it down, and drag to ground with it, moreover, the
entire gang of whores and parasites — why look at them
behind them banisters there—!

> *More shouts of* 'Hallelujah' *and other cries* — 'Pull it down
> and heave 'em out of it — strip the whores and whip their
> backs for 'em—!' *etc.*

MOTHER BUMROLL (*against the background of the shouts*).
Help help — milord, help — there's larceny and battery towards!
Get out of it, girls, quick, get out through t'back door —

> *Girls are squealing. Benches etc. are overturned.*

GRIP (*in an instant restoring quiet*). Stop! Nay nay, this is no
good. This is not what I want you to do. This is not the Lord's
work. For God's sake, think on. Expose to public chastisement
half-a-dozen weak young draggle-tails that the Constables
could ha' dealt with atween morning-prayer and breakfast. . .?
My friends, is this worthy: or is it rather a debauch no less
contemptible than that which I brought you all here to upbraid?
Aye, I said pull it down: but pull it down through the entire
land, and commence not with the most humble but with those
who from their height of duplicity and public power have
employed these works of Satan to the undoing of the true
religion! Even as they also let cruelty, injustice, greed, walk
forth like tall horses among the poor and the unenfranchised.
But a day cometh and a great reckoning. Until that time we
bide our time. Milord Grimscar, your frivolous plays have been
stopped. Our first attempt ever in this town. You are warned
by your rent-paying people not to renew them. Thomas
Backhouse, I believe you are a man of brain, so think on:
Your brimstone words upon this damnéd stage

So many years have caused the devil's brood to rage
And dance unchecked. If you make claim
That mutual intercourse is all your aim
To show folk how they live, I tell you — well:
Present to them a picture of their own living hell
And they will wallow in it, deep. Why not?
It being beyond the reach of your pale soul
To know that from this pit
There is a ladder out
And we must climb it, clamber, storm the bloodstained wall
And fight to death its keepers. I promise you we will.
Hallelujah!

Cries of 'Hallelujah'.
GRIP *leads the singing of a hymn.*

GRIP *(singing).*
'The Lord's Good Guide will walk before
His people on their Holy Road:
The Fire by night, the Smoke by day
We follow with our heavy load . . .'

The shouts and singing recede.

Scene Four

Fade out singing into exterior sounds of rain falling and rapid footsteps splashing down a wet street.

PEARL *(to herself — speech begins over end of hymn).* Myself with three terrified courtesans am hustled by Mother Bumroll into the dark street outside and the rain pouring down . . .

MOTHER BUMROLL. We tek the short cut down the ginnel, we don't stop till we get to the house — run for it, run —! Oh this town has been taken out of the hands of our Lord and master and given over to its own low rabble, we shall never again never be allowed our sweet pleasuring in decency and peace . . .

Cross fade to . . .

Interior. Rain heard faintly perhaps on window or roof.

PEARL *(to herself)*. We go in, we make all safe —

Door slamming.

We're not in her house scarce five minutes nor six when who comes but that damned clergyman. Oh, sure I had enticed him, but — he grabs hold of a black bottle, swallows it empty to the dregs: pushes aside the squawking harlots, despite the protests of the old woman, he drags me up without one word into the inner room beyond, and there he fumbles and he tumbles till behind us at the doorway she can at last get a word in edgewise —

MOTHER BUMROLL. She came in on the carrier's wagon only this morning from Liverpool, look, Parson, I'm telling you — she's a lovely young lass, but Parson she's not for you! Least not in the way you're hoping for. Her name is —

SOWSE *(drunk but not incoherent)*. Her name shall be Rahab of the scarlet thread — Biblical — oh this day has been most abject for me — I seek Lethe, young woman!

PEARL. My name is Pearl.

MOTHER BUMROLL. Don't you see?

SOWSE *(vaguely)*. Orient Pearl . . .?

PEARL. Occident.

SOWSE. What?

PEARL. I have come, Dr Sowse, from the west.

SOWSE *(disconcerted)*. Oh . . . aha, ha! You had thought I had forgotten . . .
Pearl is bright and Pearl is dark
We lodge our jewel in the walled green park.

PEARL. I don't know what the devil you imagine you mean by that, but —

SOWSE. I mean disappointment. Unendurable frustration of my immediate carnal need.

PEARL. I have come here with a message. It is secret and it's politic, it's important and incriminating: so very much so indeed that I'm not even informed what way I am to get it to the man who will take delivery; except first through Mother Bumroll, and she tells me next the Parson, and begod the Parson's drunk, and —

SOWSE. Very venially mistook you for that which you appeared.
I did advise you, Mrs Bumroll, such disguise was not prudent.

MOTHER BUMROLL. Oh aye and what's wrong with it? How
else could a female woman all on her own travel over this wild
countryside without servants nor gentlemen and no questions
to be asked? 'Cos you know what a question'd mean! A sight
worse nor a bloody back at t'cart's-tail in t'market place — it's
York Castle and a State Trial for High Treason —

SOWSE. The hangman's gallows—!

MOTHER BUMROLL. For the like o' what *she's* here for! Oh
lovey lovey I do beg you to be careful — I've been flogged five
times already, even that just once more'd burst my poor old
heart, oh Parson I'm an old woman, I could never stand it in
this world —

SOWSE. Shut your mouth and contain yourself. She must be rid
of these rags of harlotry. You have a pawnshop next door,
search your cupboards and bring out of them a black gown and
white linen, and every inch of her bold hair to be covered with
a proper kerchief. Away with you, look sharp!

MOTHER BUMROLL. Right, Parson.

Door opens.

All right, Parson, right . . .

Door closes.

SOWSE. And now, my dark-faced Rahab, d'you suppose that I
am sober?

PEARL. I wouldn't say so.

SOWSE. Oh yes I am. I will tell you for example where you came
from. First from Scotland then from Ireland and you come to
a man called Grimscar, right or wrong? You might as well
answer me, since it is I that must bring you to him. And you
might as well tell me some of the news from outside England,
which is no more than a traveller's courtesy.

PEARL. Very well. They think in Scotland that the Calvinist
Sectarians are preparing war against the King for the freedom
of their religion.

SOWSE. I had heard so. And in Ireland?

PEARL. In Ireland it is thought that the King's Lord Deputy at
   Dublin Castle is preparing a large army to be brought over to
   withstand the Scots.
SOWSE. We are aware here of the King's Lord Deputy. He is a
   local man and well-thought-upon. He owns a coalmine over
   the moors, and a great mansion-house ten miles away at the
   top end of the dale.
PEARL. You say well-thought-upon?
SOWSE. Yes. Though my Lord Grimscar cannot abide him: he
   has laid out mortgages, ten thousand pound, to gobble up
   Grimscar's land.

   Door opens.

MOTHER BUMROLL. I've brought the clothes.
SOWSE. Let her put them on. I am taking her with me at once.
MOTHER BUMROLL. Who's to pay for them?
SOWSE. You have received from me the sum total of seventeen
   pound six-and-eightpence.
MOTHER BUMROLL. Aye, for her carriage from the Liverpool
   packet: but there was nowt said about new clothes! It'll run
   to at least a guinea-and-a-half —

   Clink of coins.

SOWSE. Four half-sovereigns. Give me a receipt but don't give
   change. Your young woman in the front parlour — fat Alice or
   perhaps Betty with the bad teeth, I require one of them at
   once for my immediate carnal need. Come.

   Door slams as he goes out with MOTHER BUMROLL.

PEARL *(to herself).*
   They go out, they leave the clothes
   Tumbled all over the bed and none too clean;
   And here in the small stinking room
   Full of smoke, I must put them on,
   With six inches of cracked looking-glass
   By the light of one brothel-house candle I am left all alone;
   The glistering wig pulled off my head
   My own short hair beneath like charcoal, and my tread

Upon the floorboard heavy as lead.
I must be five-and-twenty years of age, I guess:
For a whole cold twelve of them, no less,
I have known naught but great unkindliness
I have known naught but to be always driven
Five thousand miles, God help me, under heaven . . .
I stand here bolt upright stripped to my brown skin.
I turn over and over one question: just who I am,
Who is the one who is thinking my thoughts,
Who is this woman who turns and turns at the mill of my brain?
And yet how unreasonably exalted would I find myself now
had I only been able to see the murder of Julius Caesar right
through to the end! Tantalus, ah Tantalus, and don't tell me,
that beastly clergyman, wouldn't he feel just the same about
me . . .? For each several one of us, our immediate carnal
need, perhaps today for the first time I have truly discovered
my own . . .
Who would have dreamed my brimstone blood would rage
At dance of so-called devils upon a stage,
Who performed no more than I have often done?
Yet never before did I so yearn and groan
In hope one day to set to them their tune —
Just so, I have been told,
Young girls for love of men grow hot and cold
And wriggle beneath the moon and cannot sleep.
Leave it alone: this dream will keep.
My only business now is change my shape . . .

    Fade down.

Scene Five

Fade up.

PEARL. Dr Sowse! I am quite ready! Is my appearance demure
and sober? Unexpectedly indeed, so is his. I ride on his horse
behind him through the mud and rain . . .

Quick clatter of horse hooves.

. . . to a great park-gate, through the gate to the hall of
Grimscar. Oh a big house, but so bare. Broken windows.
Cobwebs. In a small bedroom, my lord's poet. And spread
out upon the unmade bed, my lord in his boots and spurs.

Cut to . . .
Interior. Door shuts.

GRIMSCAR. Ah, Sowse. You have kept me waiting. Did you
settle the expenses?

SOWSE. [Seventeen-pound six-and-eight, as I told you, my lord:
in addition to that, two guineas, for the requisite change of
raiment.

GRIMSCAR. Two guineas? You were over-charged. One pound
ten would have been sufficient.

SOWSE. The old woman strikes a hard bargain.

GRIMSCAR. Her receipt: give it to me. Take twenty sovereigns
out of that cashbox: there you are, you are reimbursed.

Coins taken out of metal box.

BACKHOUSE [(*his speech is now brisk and abrupt*). Give the lady
the other chair.

GRIMSCAR. At the far side of the bed, where the candle can
strike on her face. I want to *see* her under that kerchief.

Chair moved.]

Very good, Sowse, you may go.

Door opens, footsteps out, door shuts.

Your name is Pearl? . . . Nothing more? . . . I repeat, have you
no more names?

PEARL. At least five. Different times, different places. They are
not to be used here: and particularly not in the presence of a
third person.

GRIMSCAR. Mr Backhouse is an old friend: his opinion is
cardinal in all my affairs. He is to be trusted as myself.

BACKHOUSE. She comes direct here from Waterford. Shall we
start off with the Irish business? Direct into it, lady, if you
don't mind: it's getting late.

PEARL. Yes . . . The King's Lord Deputy is preparing a large
    army to be brought over to withstand the —
GRIMSCAR. No. Oh no, not good enough. Already well-known.
    You have not, with so many elaborate precautions, come over
    here to tell me *that* . . . *(Quite a long pause.)* Look, we cannot
    just sit here and inform each other of nothing.
BACKHOUSE. She is trembling. She is afraid.
GRIMSCAR. I have assured you you can trust me . . . Very well
    then: I suppose I must go a deal further than I had wished.
    I must deliver myself into your hands. The Lord Deputy is my
    enemy. He is also the enemy of all those who would restore
    our English Parliament and re-establish its old curb upon the
    power of the Crown. I believe that the army he raises in Dublin
    is intended not only to coerce the rebellious Scots, but to be
    used within England for the oppression of the entire kingdom.
BACKHOUSE. We believe that the King, and the Lord Deputy,
    and the Archbishop, have in mind to erect a tyranny in this
    land that will destroy all English freedom until the old age of
    our great-grandchildren.
GRIMSCAR. And I mean, if I can, to lay waste this huge Lord
    Deputy, and to utterly root out the conspiracy that he has
    bred. So now, girl, you know my purposes. With one word
    you could put the King's axe against my neckbone. Enjoy, if
    you will, the power that you have over me —
BACKHOUSE. Over us.
GRIMSCAR. — but for God's sake tell me the truth.
PEARL *(after a short pause: in a sudden outburst)*. Death. Blood.
    Burning. Warfare. Rebellion. Determined already. Prepared-for.
    Equipped.
GRIMSCAR. In Ireland?
PEARL. *[The northern province. Where the King's Protestants,
    English and Scots, have been planted in the lands taken by
    force from the Catholic people. Towards Derry of Saint
    Columb-kill, that you Englishmen will call London's Derry,
    towards Dungannon, Donegal, Enniskillen, Strabane, the
    Bannside. It has been said, a day cometh, a great reckoning.

          *See Appendix A

The people of God will destroy in their thousands the P
of God. The Lady Eire, it has been said, will walk barefo
the mountains in her mantle of bright green.

GRIMSCAR. The names of the great men involved?

PEARL. The O'Neills are at the head of it. It is their chief, O'N
himself, on whose behalf I am sent to you, so I know. Then t
O'Donnells, the O'Dohertys, the O'Cahans, Maguires —

BACKHOUSE. In point of fact every dispossessed Catholic Gaelic
clan in the north parts.

PEARL. In point of fact. And moreover they have hope they will
be able to bring in with them the men of the west — as the
O'Flahertys of Connemara — they are my people there, I have
talked to them: they are in fear of what will happen, but if
they think it is like to succeed, then they will join.

GRIMSCAR. We had reports there was something after this
manner in preparation: but how much we have underestimated!

BACKHOUSE. I thought maybe a few skirmishes, a few dangerous
small cattle-raids —

GRIMSCAR. But this that you have told us of is nothing less than
mortal war!

PEARL.
For mortal war they swear they will not end
Until the land has been regained
From head to foot, from side to bleeding side
And lives once more a fruitful loving bride
And mother to her children —
They have convinced themselves beyond denial
Starvation breasts at once will be made full
Only because distracted brave O'Neill
Sees nothing else to do but kill
And kill and kill and kill and kill . . .
I ask you, through whose fault we have been driven to it,
whose is the fault?

GRIMSCAR. There is no need to weep at it, it is too soon, we
discuss politics, we explore technique . . .

BACKHOUSE. If we are passionate, there will be errors made.
Lady, there will be errors, we over-run ourselves: we will all
fall down!

rage). We will not. We explore technique.
quite true. My people, you see, have
great lord, from the upper house of
at, have very lately made alliance with
ans and the persecuted extreme Puritans in
at right? From what I saw this afternoon, the
n Puritans have by no means made alliance with

That was unfortunate.

USE. It is not altogether quite so bad as it appeared, but —
But you have not yet persuaded them that you are
numbered among the elect?

GRIMSCAR. I have not yet persuaded them that religion and justice and liberty *and* true poetry can all of them be one and the same thing. Forget it.

PEARL. Very well. So about Scotland. The King's Protestants in Ireland are very many of them Scots, very many of them Presbyterian. But strange, they are *not* conjoined with their brethren in Scotland to take up arms against the King. Have you considered why not? In Scotland there is contention about church-government between the Bishops and the disciples of John Knox — two sorts of Protestant: and all of them Scotsmen born. Whereas in Ireland the Protestants are for the most part new-come foreigners: and they are to this extent unanimous — they are aware of but one adversary and he is the Pope of Rome. They will give support to anyone who will protect them against Rome: even the King's Lord Deputy, though he is hand-in-hand with the King's Bishops, is yet seen as a class of Protestant and therefore they call him their friend — they are loyal men to the Crown of England.

GRIMSCAR. Yet when the King shall send the Deputy with an Army to attack the Scots, will they not then cease to be loyal?

PEARL. Wouldn't you know that already the Lord Deputy has taken good care of it? Every day all over the country his lawyers out of Dublin, with their blue bags full of forged documents, are on the prowl among the Catholics, among the Irishmen born, even those who have made sure to submit themselves to government, — and every day the Catholic lands

are most plausibly sequestrated, gobbled up and given over
into the hands of good Protestants.

GRIMSCAR. Oh he plays the same game here with the estates of
other people. I have experience —

PEARL. I have been told. And moreover, if any Protestants dare
presume to doubt the steadfastness of the King's Deputy — as
for example it has been noted that this great army of his
contains a large number of Catholic mercenaries —

BACKHOUSE. So not all of your Papists are rebels . . .?

PEARL. They can't afford to be: they must eat: and a royal
soldier gets regular pay . . . At all events, for whatever reason,
if the Protestants mistrust the Deputy, what else need he do
but quietly remind them that O'Neill has been abiding in exile
in *Madrid:* and at the slightest sign of wavering in the
Protestant loyalty, the King of Spain will invade Ireland.

GRIMSCAR. And will he?

PEARL. He will not, of course. The King of Spain is not
interested. His great Armada was made driftwood of more
than fifty years ago. And O'Neill is well aware of it. He lives in
Spain because he has to. They'd chop off his head if he came
back home openly. But when he does come, he'll come home
by himself. He has no chance of bringing an army with him.
As friends to his people, oh the Spaniards have proved
worthless . . . So he seeks for assistance elsewhere. My lord,
he seeks for it *here*. He has heard the English people demand
liberty and justice in accord with the most ancient principles
of Christian Brotherhood.

BACKHOUSE. Protestant Brotherhood.

PEARL. *Popular* Brotherhood: in opposition to the King. He
likewise observes the Scotsmen in opposition to the power of
the King. He says, for God's sake what shall hinder us to bring
all three parties together? He says, how far in truth is *religion*
the root cause of all this broil? Surely, he says, it is land, and
outrageous taxation, and the right to self-government, and
land again, land, which has been stolen from all the people —!

BACKHOUSE. Wait on, now wait a minute: now let's get this
clear. They have sent you into England to ask disaffected
English Protestants to take up the cause of the Catholics in Ireland?

GRIMSCAR. No it won't do. The Irish Catholics are determined upon massacre, you have said so — the murder and massacre of hundreds and hundreds of Protestants —!

PEARL. Hippocleides third Marquess Grimscar, if we are passionate, there will be errors made . . . O'Neill is no more of a barbarian than you are, whatever you may have been told of him. He seeks only to *prevent* massacre, by means of politics, if that is possible. For he knows if he is forced to go into his war without friends, then destruction upon Ireland for evermore and no remedy . . .

BACKHOUSE. My lord, I believe this is not quite improbable. Will you write to O'Neill? Put it clear to him: politics. Resolution of the religious differences can be left on one side for a matter of years if need be —

PEARL. Will you write to him?

GRIMSCAR. Commit my treason to pen and ink? Are you mad?

PEARL. Let you dictate a letter: I will put it into Irish and then reverse it into an agreed cipher. He will reply in the same manner. I am instructed to remain here and interpret the reply when it comes. Among your household in these garments I will not be conspicuous.

BACKHOUSE. Lady, in these garments you are the absolute and complete country-cousin of the Reformed Religion; why, you could be the god-daughter of Gideon Grip! Not a visitor to the house but will commend my lord's chastity for his acquaintance with such an one! No difficulty I suppose about conveyance of the letter?

GRIMSCAR. Dr Sowse will arrange something.

BACKHOUSE. I mistrust Dr Sowse. Do you tell me you still think him reliable?

GRIMSCAR. He has too much on his conscience to be anything else. Tom, you and I will discuss this letter alone, and then as you know, I have business. (*As he moves to the door.*) We will leave the lady here, if she does not object to the unseemly state of the bedroom.

BACKHOUSE (*following him*). As it happens, my bedroom. Oh by the way, you never told us what the Scotsmen said to your project?

PEARL. They said they would do nothing towards Ireland until they heard what would England do. They said the indolent vain Lord Grimscar was not like to do anything about anywhere, whatever: none the less they would wait for him.

> GRIMSCAR *gives a baffled bark*, BACKHOUSE *laughs. They go out and the door shuts.*

Scene Six

PEARL (*to herself, after a pause*). And in the meantime *I* must wait for him. For three hours, four hours until it is near midnight.] There are books in this bedroom, for amusement. Books of plays. Book of the play 'Julius Caesar'. I read page after page of it, and so much more than amusement . . . intense preoccupation, and at last, of a sudden, broken —

> *Door open.*

BACKHOUSE. Are you coming? We'll find our suppers. They'll be laid for us, private, at the corner of the great hall. There'll be no-one else at table . . .

> *Their feet echo hollow down stairs, along passages.*

He's no more than the two-three servants left him in the whole of his house, so we find our own way. Watch your feet on the stair. That's your bedroom, through the arch, for when you want to go to it . . . Destruction upon Ireland . . . for evermore and no remedy . . . upon England as well: not so much the body and bones — deeper, within the soul . . . there's few can foresee it but me, very like: but then I've been into Ireland. Oh no further than Kilkenny, with Jack Barnabas and his actors on tour: but I saw what I saw . . . dilapidation, deracination, the gangrene of conquest and greed . . . I saw there the end of all manner of good nature. Oh there's too much of good nature in this house at present. Hippocleides Lord Grimscar brim-full of abundant nature in his own

quarters in the west wing is entertaining female company . . .
Do you not want to know whose?

PEARL. None of my business.

BACKHOUSE (*as distant lute-music becomes evident*). Oh I think
it very well might be. She arrived here in a golden coach about
an hour before you did. She is the Countess Belladonna, a
widow-woman of great fortune and most sumptuous appetite.
She has offered my lord hope for the redemption of his estate,
which you'll have noticed is in grave need of it. In return, you
see, she would entangle him into her political faction — I mean
the faction of the King and his Court against Parliament:
which is dangerous, if she can do it. Wouldn't you say? Oh no
doubt he can take her and leave her — I *hope* . . . good nature
and abundant wantonness. Notwithstanding, she does have
influence. My lord's acclaimed patronage of players and poets
comes largely from her strong-box. Indirectly, she feeds me,
and the lute-strings and wandering fingers up there behind the
oriel window are adding up, you might say, the bill-of-
reckoning for our own small supper . . .

> *Door opens and shuts. They walk into the hall, with a new
> quality of echo, and the music is shut off with the door.*

. . . Which is what? Lentil porridge: and we sit down to it off
two stools on a cold flagstone . . .

> *Stools scrape as they sit.*

Tuck that blanket round your feet, lass, the draught over this
floor's mortal . . . what's this then?

PEARL. I'd call it a bottle.

BACKHOUSE. So would I. But what's in it? Go on, taste it and
tell me.

> *Glug glug.*

PEARL. Aqua-vitae. Begod, that's good.

BACKHOUSE. Don't drink all of it. Give back a libation to the
giver of all good things . . .

> *Glug glug.*

BACKHOUSE.
> Aha . . .
> Begod, as you put it, that's good.
> Spirit of warm cordial at back of your two black eyes
> Like arising of birds' wings in the deep of a thick wood . . .
> For the first time since you came here, aye look at me, return
>   my gaze,
> There is that in your closed dark countenance that seems to
>   have summat to say
> That you yourself have your own choice person, you have your
>   own private heart and it beats blood.
> Irish eyes are not dead black? I would ha' thought more like
>   green-gray . . .?

PEARL. Who said I was Irish?

BACKHOUSE. You did. Connemara. You said the people were your people.

PEARL. So they are. But I can't claim that I altogether am one of theirs. I speak their language, about as well as I speak your English, I mean as it were sideways. My mother was a concubine to one of the chieftains there, O'Flaherty. He would make raids upon the Galway merchants. The Lord Deputy's dragoons were sent into the mountains to punish him. They burnt and they killed and they captured. They tied a rope round the neck of my mother and the other end to a trooper's horse, they dragged her naked through the winter — oh no, not her alone, a whole wretched crowd of them, weeping and bleeding — till they came to a ship tied up at a stone pier where there were stone warehouses and a fortified bridge and a row of cannon in front of the bridge to keep the O'Flahertys from getting them back. And there, under the east wind in a storm of sleet and rain, the auctioneer of Galway City stood on a tub and roared out for his price. They were all sold to a gang of merchants who entrusted them to the ship's captain, who at once hoisted sail, with his crammed cargo, for the new-found land.

BACKHOUSE. The American Plantations?

PEARL.
> Virginia. It had been given that name —

For purity and growth and hope:
This place of chains and whips and misery and rape.

They sold my mother to a man who had fields, as he called
them, where he intended to plant tobacco. They were not
fields, they were forest. They were cleared into fields by a long
line of people, chained together, black and white. They cut
down trees and scrabbled out the heavy stumps. They chopped
the earth flat with mattocks. She had been there I suppose six
months, when the red men came out of the forest. They burnt
and they killed and they captured. They tied a rope round the
neck of my mother: they dragged her naked through the
thickets and swamps till they came to the place where they
lived. Thatched cabins all surrounded by a palisade of
sharpened timber. She said, only for the stone tower of the
O'Flahertys, she might have thought herself in Connemara.
Indeed she became a concubine to one of the chief men of the
tribe: nothing new for her in that, but this time she gave birth
to a child. Me.
She was held at the end in high honour and regard
For the good sense and affection she gave back as reward
To him who had taken her, that he did not take her life.
She wore a blanket of red wool, carried a short bone-handled
   knife —
Here it is —
BACKHOUSE. Carved and beautiful, a deadly jewel at your own
belt.
PEARL.
   It is all I have left to remember her by,
   To remember my tall dark father, how his murderous black
      eyes would melt
   At the sight of my mother and me
   Playing and laughing in the long glade
   That led out of our village into the heart of the unknown wood.
   Don't put your finger on the edge of that blade:
   I have used it to cut through a man's throat.
BACKHOUSE. And so what happened?

PEARL.
  My breasts were already grown when my life like a man's cut
     throat
  Split into two: and was never from that time mended.
  Nor can it be till all is ended . . .

  The white men came out of the forest. They burnt and they
  killed and they captured. I will tell you no detail: except that
  this knife, in my hand as you now see it, gained a secret
  revenge, again and again, for the things that they did to my
  mother.
BACKHOUSE. That who did? The white men? They were English?
PEARL. What else? She was a red man's wife and glad of it: she'd
  given over her religion and bent her head to the gods of an
  heathen. And even had she not, don't you know she'd have
  been a Papist?
BACKHOUSE. And *your* religion? Have you got one?
PEARL. As the faith of my mother in the Virgin the Mother of
  God; or the faith of my father in the wild spirits of the rivers
  and trees and the beasts of the new-found land . . .? How much
  of conviction in all this for a woman like me, for where I am,
  for what I am doing, for where I have been, for what I have
  seen there . . .?
BACKHOUSE. And so what happened then?
PEARL. I worked my passage, don't they call it? At all events
  fought for it. Then year after year, ever changing my shape,
  back to Europe from the New World a Conquistador in reverse,
  discovering everything I could, from whomever was so foolish
  as to permit me to look into their business. In the end I got
  back to that ill-omened small island beside Europe where my
  mother had been bought and sold: until one morning with my
  own eyes I glared up at the brass cannon on the fort-bridge of
  Galway. After that: so here I am. Is there anything left at the
  bottom of your bottle?
BACKHOUSE. Take it . . . So that's your story. I don't know.
  Do I believe you? Or do I convince myself that for some reason
  you have invented me a romantic impertinent fable for one of
  my plays?

PEARL. Credulous or incredulous, I don't give a damn.

BACKHOUSE. Yet it is no more fantastical than the proposition
you put to Grimscar. Good God he was bewildered by it. If he
really were to confederate the Papist malignants abroad with
the Protestant rebels at home, there too would be matter for a
remarkable strange play. Why, Cassius and his conspirators
would be nothing to it, I can tell you — pit and gallery of all
England would be shook like a watchman's rattle!

PEARL. Do you always consider everything in terms of the stage?

BACKHOUSE. Aye, I'm bound to: it's my trade . . . I am made
sick by the state of my trade.

PEARL. I don't know why. You are not an actor. In those parts
of the world where it is permitted to females, *I* have performed,
I know what I'm talking about, I had no choice, I must travel,
I must earn a living — but out of what? Such miserable mean
extemporary botching that we stitched and we patched into
some sort of grace with the jerk of our loins and the rotation of
of our armpits — we called them *plays*. Had it been possible to
have had written for us a true play by a true poet, like the one
this afternoon —

BACKHOUSE (*sardonic*). You'd have felt yourself honoured to
assist at so marvellous a mystery?

PEARL. I would so: and without sarcasm.

BACKHOUSE. Same thoughts as I had once — over twenty years
ago — in the yard of a public inn under the shadow of
Beverley Minster: there was a scaffold built, six feet high,
painted cloths hung up behind with the sun and the moon
and the stars of the Zodiac in silver and gold against blue:
and Jack Barnabas in the middle of it, a huge plume to his hat
and a sword at his side, he was Romeo, he was in love. And his
boy-Juliet, when she came to him, pale-faced and thin, her
long legs stirring the folds of her gown more enchantingly than
any real woman I had ever seen in my life, and her voice like a
nightingale. That's for me, I said: aye: my trade, I'll never give
over. No more I have. But where did it get me? Belladonna the
opulent Countess, and her cormorant companions, swallowing
up the entire commonwealth, demanding nothing from their
poets but to make a scarecrow out of honest men, abuse the

citizens, flatter the courtiers, run like a rabbit from all mention of public affairs!

He gets up, pushes his stool back, strides across the floor, opens the door. The lute music is heard again.

PEARL. But sure Grimscar does not want —

BACKHOUSE. Hippocleides Marquess Grimscar has no notion of what he wants. He makes politics to please the Puritans, he has plays written to enkindle his whore. Good night!

His footsteps stamping away down the passage.

PEARL *(to herself)*. Aye aye, my trade — aye — [that's for *me!*] Sure I have seen it and heard it, I will never give over — if only I can once find the way to begin . . .

Fade out.

Scene Seven

Fade in — lute music brought up loud. Interior. Clatter of cutlery and glasses as if a meal is being cleared from a table onto a tray and placed aside.

BELLADONNA *(singing to the lute).*
   'I had a husband once did please
   Me every way but one
   He cruelly left me seek my ease
   In naked bed alone . . .'

   Red wine, at my expense, for my dear heart Hippocleides, roast goose, at my expense — has not your desire even yet been aroused by the ingestion of these good gifts . . .?

   (Sings again.)
   'But now he's dead, his gold is mine
   Each guinea of his making —
   He left to me enough, thank God,
   To keep the widow waking.'

GRIMSCAR. I tell you they would have sat through the whole

play and applauded it, had Grip not appeared in their midst —

BELLADONNA. [At least you had the good sense not to offer those stone-brained wool-weavers some cuckoldy comedy from the hand of your man Backhouse, fleering and jeering at the Puritan hypocrisy —

GRIMSCAR. I was told Grip was out of town, gone to Hull, I was informed, to look at a shipload of timber. Oh I do not understand his most damnable intransigence: I am recognized as a whole-hearted defender of these people against enclosures, immoderate taxes, and the interference of the Archbishop, yet nevertheless —]

BELLADONNA. Nevertheless Gideon Grip is possessed of the people's allegiance, and you, Hippocleides, are not. Why, the man should be locked-up, not protected, you damfool: for what else are you called a great lord? You were born to command in this kingdom, to be obeyed, and to thrive at it. Yet you wilfully betray your obligations to your own party, you look to be accepted by their envious opponents, and you weep upon my knee when they tell you what they think of you.

GRIMSCAR. Belladonna, five years ago I was indeed of your party. And those whom you know well manoeuvred me out of a monopoly I was promised, and an appointment of profit guaranteed at the King's elbow: I was induced to venture money in an American plantation which failed, and which we both know too damned well was intended to fail. Do you ask me to league myself yet again with such rascals? I won't do it . . .! Why do you come here?

BELLADONNA. Out of frantic desire, the lechery of my marrow-bones, because I can't keep away from you. Hippocleides, undo the laces at the top of my sleeves, Hippocleides listen to me, when had you last sufficient money to present a complete new play, composed by your own poet, dressed and decorated according to your own most improvident taste, equipped with new music and moveable scenes, and performed by the best actors to be found in the whole of London?

GRIMSCAR. A great many years ago, I did use to —

BELLADONNA. You did use to: you don't any more, there is a

framework to this gown, you'll find a knot in the tape here
and another one down there to secure it to the whalebone,
undo them without tugging at them, that's right, Hippocleides,
I am falling into a delirium of unrequited generosity:
Hippocleides, what could you not do with the banqueting-hall
of my mansion upon the London Strand: suppose you were to
present there, at my expense, a dramatic entertainment more
splendid than anything since the days of Heliogabalus — shall
we say for the night of your birthday, which is far enough
ahead to give everyone concerned sufficient time for all
arrangements? Aha, . . . haha . . . the fish is hooked — I know
that your lust for the pomp and passion of a stage play was
ever ten times more nervous than for the curvatures of my
white body . . . It is agreed? Or do you fear it will destroy
your friendship with your cold-nosed whey-faced political
associates?

GRIMSCAR. They are already well-informed of my pleasures,
Belladonna, both theatrical and venereal. I make no bones of
them. I am determined that the party opposed to the King
shall be seen to encompass far more than sectarian exclusivism.
We are in business to preserve the ancient liberties of all
England: toleration of my own liberty is a *sine qua non.*

BELLADONNA. Rubbish, roll down my stockings, there is no
person will tolerate your liberty save me.

GRIMSCAR. And not even you, were it not for the hazard you
might procure my voice in Parliament against the enemies of
the King . . .?

BELLADONNA. Rubbish, there is no Parliament: the King will
rule upon his own till the day of the Last Trumpet.

GRIMSCAR. Will he? Did you not know that His Majesty all of a
sudden is in very hard case for the exceeding deficiency of the
revenue he had hoped to obtain?

BELLADONNA. The revenue withheld from him,
contumaciously, by such as you!

GRIMSCAR. Be that as it may, he is about to recall Parliament.

BELLADONNA (*suddenly very serious*). Is this true?

GRIMSCAR. I had a messenger this morning from Pontefract.
Oh yes it is quite true. And which way will I vote in the

Parliament, Belladonna? Forget about your goddamned play.
I am no longer to be bought and sold! Do you not understand?

BELLADONNA. I understand it too damned well, except at the
one huge price, my hand in marriage, is it not? And you
certainly don't get *that*. I give away only so much of my
fortune as is convenient for my immediate desire. I have
already told you my immediate desire. [Hand me your
instrument, I will sing you some more of the same old song,
let us both understand where we are —

(She sings to the lute.)
'I can please you whene'er I choose
And choose you when I please
Hang silver rings around your neck
And help you seek your ease —']

Dear heart, is it agreed, in my house upon the Strand upon
your birthday, it is agreed . . . Are there not so many new
glories of the art of Roscius you have longed for years to
introduce? For example, out of Italy, the use of women upon
the stage . . .?

GRIMSCAR. This is a play not a masque, it is contrary to the
custom, it will not be approved.

BELLADONNA. In a private house, at my expense, I have no
doubt it will be permitted . . . My God, if there is to be a
Parliament, I must leave for London first thing in the
morning —

(Sings to the lute.)
'My body in your naked bed
Till then is for the taking
We do not need a lawyer's deed
To keep the widow waking . . .'

Hippocleides, dear heart, do exactly whatever you want . . .

Fade out.

Scene Eight

*Exterior. Morning birdsong. Sounds of harnessed coach-horses
fidgeting as they wait.*

PEARL *(to herself)*. At last after so many weeks a reasonable soft
bed and for a novelty I am crouched-upon by no bad dreams.
The sensation at long last I have occasion to do exactly
whatever I please . . In the cold sunshine on the terrace, below
the steps of the great hall-door, an elaborate carriage is waiting.
Three people upon the threshold. The lady is bidding farewell
to my lord. She is garnished as brave as a maypole: opening up
a rat-trap smile over her shoulder towards Backhouse, who
takes care not to seem to return it . . .

BACKHOUSE *(sardonic)*. It can be done. Oh it can be done, aye,
of course I can make a play to have women in it, half-trained,
painted scenery and what not, new-fangled for my lord's
birthday, why not from a man of my age, get in first and pull
out the floorboards from under the feet of these new young
cleverdicks? Why not?

BELLADONNA. There you are, Hippocleides, I told you he
would be jubilant. Mr Backhouse: your invention has always
excelled far beyond any fantasy of your younger and more
fashionable rivals . . .
(With a sudden change of tone.) Hippocleides, who is this?

PEARL *(to herself)*. She is looking up at me as I stand in the
porch of the hall: and I look at her. This is not the first time
I have seen her. Who is she . . .?

BELLADONNA *(spiteful)*. Your eccentric political allegiance,
Hippocleides, will no doubt account for your choice of a
housekeeper — sub-fusc, is she not, like your own self while at
home in Yorkshire? Madam Prudence-in-the-pantry — is that
her name, hey, baptised with the distilled waters of a Geneva
Conventicle? Rubbish, within her Puritan kerchief she has the
complexion of a black-moor: and they sing no metrical psalms
in Tangier that ever I heard of.

GRIMSCAR. Belladonna, you go beyond yourself. She is — she is
the mistress of my poet, who else could she be? Goddamit,
Tom, did you tell me her name or didn't you?

BACKHOUSE *(suppressed exasperation)*. I did tell you, yesterday.
Her name is Margery, my lord, and she comes from —

BELLADONNA. I don't give a cod from the devil where she
comes from. Nor yet whether 'tis you that she sleeps with
when I'm not here or Backhouse every night of the month.

> *She goes, feet crunching on gravel, and mounting into the
> coach.*

PEARL *(to herself)*. She is into her coach, the groom's up
behind, the coachman holds ready his whip — she has her head
out of the window for one last farewell message —

BELLADONNA. Hippocleides, tell your housekeeper that when
I put my hand under your thigh, it is a fulcrum to turn over
the world!

> *As she speaks this the coach gets going with a great deal of
> noise.*

GRIMSCAR *(starts to speak before the rattle of the vehicle has
died away — urgent and breathless)*. Now I have to get to
London before she does, is it possible? If the Parliament is to
be recalled, I have to talk to men about it in York and in
Nottingham before I get there, by God I shall be riding day
and night till the horse dies under me. I have drafted the
letter to O'Neill, girl, here it is. It says *Yes:* so you should be
pleased. Don't answer me, I'm in a hurry. Translate it and give
it to Sowse. He knows in what manner it will need to be
dispatched. Tom: while I'm away, this goddamned new play
must be completed: make sure it's good. God in heaven, after
all these years we have a Parliament at Westminster once
more — what can we not do with it!

BACKHOUSE. You'll be lucky if you do any more than you did
with it the last time.

GRIMSCAR. There is one thing we must do! We must at once get
a bill drafted that never again never can the Crown dissolve
Parliament without the consent of both our Houses!

BACKHOUSE. You intend to commence business with a bill that
says *that*, why, the King will be beside himself —

GRIMSCAR. He will know that the time has come to make his

one fatal choice: himself or the English people! Hello there —
where's my boots! Where's my horse! I'm to be on the road in
five minutes . . .!

   Fade out.

Scene Nine

Back inside the hall.

PEARL. She has been sometimes in France, that extensive gay
   lady?
BACKHOUSE.*(surly)*. Aye: she's well-travelled. Both by coach
   and by bedstead. Why d'you ask?
PEARL. Because I think I saw her there, six months ago, at a
   convent of nuns, near Dijon.
BACKHOUSE. A convent! By God, there must have been fog on
   the roads that night.

   Sound of stools as they sit down.

PEARL. There was a conference there of Irishmen, political exiles
   and others, to advance their more secretive rebellious affairs.
   I had my own business on behalf of the O'Flahertys. And it
   was there that this lady was observed walking and talking in
   the garden all morning with Phelim O'Neill. He put it out she
   was a Frenchwoman, with a message from his people in Rome.
   It was believed. I now know that he told us a lie. What d'you
   make of it?
BACKHOUSE. Nothing at all. Who is this Phelim? He is not the
   clan-chief?
PEARL. A close relative. But not in agreement with the chief
   upon policy. It was rumoured he favoured support for the
   King against Parliament in return for concessions to the
   Catholic clans . . . Oho rumour . . .? No, no it is the absolute
   truth, and the Countess Belladonna has been his agent in these
   schemes.
BACKHOUSE. Truth or rumour, it makes no odds. That paper in

your hand turns every trump she holds to deuces. Read it and rake in the stakes . . .

Short pause, rustle of paper.

PEARL. You are aware of the contents of this?

BACKHOUSE. Why, I drafted the bugger myself. Summat wrong with it?

PEARL. Only that I scarcely believe that O'Neill can believe it. It is far and away too good. Lord Grimscar here offers, on behalf of the English Parliament —

BACKHOUSE. When the English Parliament in due course has attained its own proper sovereignty — oh the offer is highly conditional, no doubt about that.

PEARL. *[He offers to restore the complete proper sovereignty of the Four Provinces of Ireland into the hands of the Irish themselves . . . whoever they may be, whether Gaelic clans or city-burgesses, Protestant or Catholic, or what, he does not indicate . . . but even so! You do believe his associates in the Parliament will guarantee this — this heroic estimate of Anglo-Saxon generosity . . .?

BACKHOUSE. In return, as it says, for O'Neill's guarantee that he will not attack the King's Protestants in their northern settlement, but instead will devote his forces to the defence of the English Parliament against the tyranny of the Crown: if O'Neill will give us that, I think Parliament will refuse him nothing.

PEARL. Not even the toleration throughout Ireland of the Catholic Church . . .? At the same time as the Presbyterians throughout Scotland are likewise tolerated . . . His Majesty the King is presently the ruler of three Kingdoms and it is he who determines the religion in each one of them. If that is taken away from him . . .

BACKHOUSE (*after a pause*). It is true that this King is described as an Anointed King. It is a sacrament: it confers upon him —

PEARL. By his own claim, I believe, divinity: yes? My father in the new-found land had a bag of medicine, as he called it.

*See Appendix B

Without that bag he would have been no chief: but an outcast
and a mark for every stone and arrow in the forest. To hurl
down your English King to the state of a naked slave, a
proclaimed runaway . . . what would you call it? A Republic?
Are you and Grimscar prepared to take all this upon
yourselves — to spill out upon the sea-shore the most
mysterious protective power of your people? Ah well, you are
an oak-timbered free-born gray-haired Englishman and no
doubt you are well aware of the boundaries of your courage.

BACKHOUSE. By the Lord . . . a Republic . . . a free Republic of
the English Commonwealth. Ah God if we must come to it,
then come to it we must! Let Grimscar take his measure of
the full implications! For if my life and his are to be laid
along the hangman's yardstick, it had best be for a prize
worth-while . . . Worth a damn sight more anyroad than this
play that he wants me to write — or *she* wants it — *I* don't
know — at the expense of my self-respect. They want nymphs
in it with round bare legs, Bacchanalians, a pair of lovers who
turn out to be brother and sister, and at the end a bloody great
rainbow and Diana coming down in a cloud. The like of what
they kept Ben Jonson fooling around with thirty years ago.
I won't have it! I'll tell him no! I'll tell him by God if anyone's
to come at the end in a cloud, what's the matter with Gideon
Grip — with his Scripture in his fist and his psalm-singing
wool-weavers behind him — every man with a good thick
cudgel! Ha, how the folk in that London *palazzo* of hers'd run
bawling for the door and hatchway! Eh dear, but it couldn't
be done . . .

PEARL. It could of course . . .

BACKHOUSE. Oh it could, but it'd be no good without Gideon
in person and all his flock among the audience — or at least
their equivalent out of the mean streets of royal London. And
you know the like of those lads'd never dream to go into a
stage play. Yet without them to cheer out their throats for me,
I find nowt any more in the whole of England fit for the tip of
my pen. Oh I could have done once — we all could — and what
happened? We threw it away, sitha! I tell you, the English stage,
whereon I've worked for a quarter-century — and don't tell me

I haven't worked well — if this stage is from now on capable of
holding only the attention of the court-harlots and their
embroidered stallions, then Jonson and Shakespeare,
Christopher Marlowe and all the rest of 'em might just as well
have spent their lives emptying nightsoil into t'village-midden.
We spoke once to the whole people. But these days we have
rejected the homespun jackets, the square-toed shoes, and the
forthright word of the godly tradesmen. And by God they've
rejected *us*. There are those in the Parliament have said openly
they'd close down every playhouse if they once attained full
power. And I *want* them to attain full power. And the whole
of my life's work will be broken in two by it . . .

PEARL. Or else altogether made new: as new as a new Republic?

BACKHOUSE. Pearl, Margery, whatever your name is,
    housekeeper, mistress, whatever your status: I am not a young
    man. Where am I to go, child, what am I to do . . .?

PEARL. This book, of the Scripture, Gideon Grip holds in his fist.
    What does it contain?

BACKHOUSE. What does it cont . . . do you mean to tell me you
    have never looked into the Bible? Why what kind of an
    upbringing have you — oh of course, you did —

PEARL. I did tell you. Are there stories in this book? I mean
    stories like of the great Romans? On the walls of the churches
    in Italy and Spain I have seen pictures and statues —

BACKHOUSE. Aye you have and they're in the book. Except of
    course for those that were made up in The Vatican. But what
    of them?

PEARL. Out of his own book an acted play: out of his own
    politics a victorious struggle. Don't you think we could find one
    for him?

BACKHOUSE. For Gideon Grip?

PEARL. You have the book?

BACKHOUSE. Oh aye, I have the book . . . Shall we go to my
    room and get it?]

Fade down.

Scene Ten

Fade up, turning pages.

PEARL (*reading*). 'Then Esther the Queen answered and said
unto the King, "We are sold, I and my people, to be destroyed,
to be slain, and to perish." ' By whom are they slain? By the
command of the King's Lord Deputy, cruel Haman, the
corrupt minister of Ahasuerus King of Persia, isn't that so?

BACKHOUSE. Aye.

PEARL (*reading*). 'Then Haman was afraid before the King and
the Queen: and they hanged Haman on the gallows that he
had prepared for Mordecai . . .' And that's it. That's what we
want. What are your writing?

> *Scratch of a pen.*

BACKHOUSE. Read me some more. I want the verses and the
chapters to connect in my head like the bones of a skeleton.
They have not yet done so. Read me, at random.

PEARL. I don't know why — in *my* head the entire body of it
already connected: it is already a golden statue three times the
height of life-size: stop scribbling on your paper and watch
her begin to walk! 'And all the king's servants, that were in the
king's gate, bowed, and reverenced Haman: for the king had so
commanded concerning him. But Mordecai bowed not, nor
did him reverence. Then was Haman full of wrath. And he
sought to destroy all the Jews that were throughout the
kingdom of Ahasuerus . . .'

Bowed not, nor did him reverence . . . as but yesterday, in the
town hall, boldly before the face of Grimscar — 'My Lord's
presence is a foul carbuncle covered over with his ermine
robe . . .' Oho, here is a story cuts forward and back both
ways . . . I said what are you writing?

BACKHOUSE. Forward and back both ways — I am already
persuaded: I have laid out the title-page: listen:
'The Brave Deeds of Godly Queen Esther for the Salvation of
her People Israel — a chronicle-history in five acts, by
T. Backhouse, gent.' And now to note down the main

argument of each act! Introduce the protagonist, fetch forward
his antagonist —

PEARL (*suddenly very cold*). I don't know those words.

BACKHOUSE. I mean Mordecai, Haman, the two great men of
the theatric conflict —

PEARL. 'Then Esther bade them return Mordecai this answer,
"I will go in unto the king, which is not according to the law:
and if I perish, I perish . . ." ' A young woman out of nothing
chosen forth by pure chance to stand all on her own bolt-
upright under peril of death to perform this great mercy — and
yet Mordecai is the 'great man' — the pro — pro —

BACKHOUSE. Protagonist . . .

PEARL. — and the full credit for presenting him goes to
T. Backhouse, gent.

BACKHOUSE (*slowly, as he understands*). Eh . . .? Oh . . . you
move your mind, young woman.

PEARL. And does *your* mind move commensurate?

BACKHOUSE (*after a pause, explosively*). How can I put your
name on it when I don't even know it? Pearl Margery,
Margery Pearl — you gave yourself the one name and the
other one comes from me!

PEARL. My true name having been given me in the forest of the
new-found land . . . where it stays, and out of sight. And of
course it would be not good sense to have it put upon an
English play. In your country in public I do not exist. Except
I should change my shape to the pretended shape of someone
else. For an instance, Queen Esther . . . You have no women
in your plays here. Therefore those that you will find for
Grimscar will be, as you told him, half-trained. I myself am
not well-trained: but I have acted with companies that would
come to a town like this one, the crude message of their work
would be *welcomed* by the carpenter, by the wool-weavers
with such exuberance that the lord and the priest would join
together to put them down. What you want for your England
I have already found elsewhere.

BACKHOUSE. For an instance, where?

PEARL. In the regions of Popery, on the shores of the
Mediterranean, where the Irish these days must wander.

BACKHOUSE. And the degree of artistry of these troupes?

PEARL. I will write out the letter into code for Dr Sowse. While I do so let you be thinking of the degree of artistry and how far it is what you require for this play. We were thieves, Mr Backhouse, and harlots, and coney-catchers, with lewd comedies, antique morality-plays, incompetent juggling, we put forward our legs in scarlet stockings and pranced around with the castanets. We were everything Jack Barnabas is not: and never would be — till you show him your play.

Fade down on scratching of pen.

Fade up — scratching of pen. It stops.

It is finished?

BACKHOUSE. End of the third act. D'you want to change it? Yet again d'you want to change it?

PEARL. Very like we will change it tomorrow.

BACKHOUSE groans.

Do I drive you too hard? Don't you think I am myself driven?

BACKHOUSE.
All by yourself, alone, in that black Puritan gown,
Like a half-starved yet sharp-toothed questing mouse,
You drive yourself alone throughout this empty house
Week after week while I sit still and write
And write the words of your desire. Have you not thought
That out of this inevitably has grown
My own gold statue of desire, body and bone,
Articulate, complete, save only for the high-crowned head . . .?

Fade out.

Scene Eleven

Fade up — distant music of a drum and tin whistle.

PEARL (*to herself*).
It was not wise to listen to what he said.

I did not that night lie in the playwright's bed.
Nor on the next, nor on the next one after,
Until the whole long tale of our bold daughter
Esther the Queen of Persia was all but made
Upon the pages as we wanted it. And then he played
Indeed, curled like a crackling hedgehog in between
My arms between the blankets from the dark till dawn.

BACKHOUSE *(half in sleep).* Oh my true sweetheart, little redskin against my chest, little cargo from the wharves of slavery, never in all my life — you know I can't say these things nigh as well as I can write them, but —

PEARL *(affectionate but sardonic).* Never in all your life . . . keep that and remember it, don't forget it for twelve months . . . By then shall we not both have made of you the poet you have always been . . .?
(To herself.)
The sun rose up. I woke, and he lay sleeping.
Slowly along the whitewashed wall came creeping
It seemed to me a picture, green, slate-blue,
Yellow like vomit, shifting, dissolving, till I scarcely knew
Whether what I saw was on the hard bare wall
Or far beyond it, as it were a tunnel
Clear through the house, the trees, the sky, the universe —
It was not like a nightmare, it was worse.
My man was sleeping, I was wide awake:
I sweated rigid in the bed and could not speak.

> *The music has come up louder and now contains additional percussion instruments, cymbals, little bells, irregularly sounding, not in conventional musical time.*

PEARL. As I remember it afterwards, it appeared to me this way — a terrible tall gaunt woman with the head of a kingfisher came wading out of the sea, under the moon, through the mudflats, onto a low green hill.

> *Wet heavy footsteps growing nearer.*

Her stark legs were striped with mud, the feathers that grew from her head extended down her bare back to the top of her

buttocks. She carried an arquebus-gun, and the match that
would fire it was burning. She turned her bird's head left-to-
right, crying out like a bird —

The footsteps stop. Single ominous bird-calls, quite loud.

— till she found what she looked for — a sort of temple,
ruined and roofless, with a heavy leather curtain hung upon
brass rings between the pillars.

Fade up the sound of a slight wind rattling curtain-rings.

She poised her arquebus, carefully took aim against the centre
of the temple-curtain, brought the match towards the touch-
hole —

MALE VOICE (BACKHOUSE's, *distorted and muffled*).
End the song, turn the tune:
The great gun shoots and all too soon.

*Gun-shot, followed immediately by a hoarse continuing
scream, a clang of arms, and then the scream comes nearer.*

PEARL *(to herself)*. The cry that I heard came from right behind
the curtain. It was dragged to one side and the shape of a man
fell out. He was in armour and he screamed. I looked into his
helmet. Dead. A dead skull. Dead and rotten five hundred
years. And the skull went on screaming, and I knew whose it
was . . .! *(Her voice rises to a yell of horror.)*

And the music and other sounds stop abruptly.

Tom, Tom, Tom — for God's sake wake up!
BACKHOUSE *(dopily)*. Hey, hey, what's the matter — sweetheart,
Margery, what has frightened you —?
PEARL. Tom, it was *your* dead face in the helmet — yours —!
BACKHOUSE. What on earth do you mean? You've been
dreaming, you've had a nightmare —
PEARL You think I have . . .? Ah yes, I was asleep, I was asleep
surely, I did dream . . .
'The great gun shoots and all too soon . . .'
Tom, I did not dream! I have been *told!* Tom, we are in great
danger, we are in danger of forgetting everything! We walk
the rooms of this house and we sit at the table and we write

and we talk, and for what purpose? To give birth to no more
than one hundred pages of words upon paper? Or to construct
a performed play that will by its very performance advance
the urgent purposes for which I am sent here: and for which
Grimscar has gone to London?

BACKHOUSE (*wearily*). Grimscar is in London to strengthen
Parliament against the Lord Deputy: you are in England to gain
Parliament's support for the grievances of O'Neill — the two
purposes are related but by no means identical. Only the first
of them will be affected by this play. What are you talking
about? Look you woke me with your nightmare: we went to
bed very late: I don't want to *stay* awake for political
controversy.

PEARL. *My* purpose will be served the better Grimscar can serve
his. We know that the Puritans are not confident of his
integrity. But the play is so powerful and unprecedented
that any Puritan who sees it will immediately reverse his
whole attitude to the English theatre. They will thoroughly
accept Grimscar as speaking through his poet with the true
voice of the common people. And when they do that, how
much more will they accept him when he presents them with
O'Neill's proposal? I safeguard my own mission with the
success of this play. So what has to be done: Tom, what must
we do now? I will tell you, and don't curl up on me under
that damned blanket. First, by whatever method, Grimscar
must get his party into Belladonna's house to be present at
the performance.

BACKHOUSE. He has promised me he will do his best —

PEARL. More than his best, by God he must succeed. Second: by
whatever method, the production must follow exactly the
manner and style we have determined for it. I do not trust
that Jack Barnabas. He is no way inclined to our political
point of view. He will never understand it, he will abhor it —
isn't that so?

BACKHOUSE. Oh Margery, look here, I have told you I can
inveigle him — he's an actor, he wants a part to display himself
in, we have written for him Haman; he reads the script, he
reads that role — he sees himself triumphant as a great

statesman of Persia, he sees himself undone by his own
unsuspected internal moral flaw: he sees the sympathy of the
audience flowing over him like hot pottage — a most poignant
classical tragedy and he won't even notice your part nor its
effect upon the meaning of the entire play from start to finish.

PEARL. He will, during the rehearsal.

BACKHOUSE. Not if you keep your mouth shut, he won't. I tell
you I know him, I can handle him. He's the best actor in
England: I will work with none other: and he *respects* me,
don't you see?

PEARL. He has no reason to respect *me*. And I am part-author of
the text. Because of me you will deceive him . . . Don't you
believe me when I say 'dangerous'?

BACKHOUSE. The whole business of Dr Sowse and the
correspondence with O'Neill is in my opinion far more
dangerous. I told Grimscar that insidious cleric ought not to
be trusted. He was asking me questions yesterday about you.
And then he was inquiring about what he termed my 'literary
labours'. What's that noise?

Knocking hard at a door.

SOWSE (*calling*). Mr Backhouse, Mr Backhouse . . .!

PEARL. Look out of the window: it sounds like the man himself.
I'll get back to my own bedroom . . .

BACKHOUSE. No — wait — see what he's come for first.

Window opened.

Dr Sowse, is that you? What kind of a time is this to be
thundering at a front door?

SOWSE (*from a distance*). Mr Backhouse, I have breakfasted . . .
Mr Backhouse, I have a letter. To be given to the — to the
housekeeper . . . Goodness me, Mr Backhouse, didn't it come
quick . . .? Will you descend, sir, and open the door?

BACKHOUSE. Directly . . .

Window shuts.

Margery, get dressed, get back to your bedroom, and be ready
to appear as though nothing had happened. We will take this
letter to London, and you will not translate it till we get there,

is that clear: because Sowse will be riding with us and he must not know what it contains. Also not one word upon the journey about the script — I will carry it privately strapped under my clothes.

PEARL. It seems to me the script has only just been completed in time.

Fade out.

Scene Twelve

Interior.

BELLADONNA. Dr Sowse, you will not prevaricate. You came here express to betray your lord and patron. Your motives are immaterial.

DR SOWSE. My lady, my motives are crucial —

BELLADONNA. Rubbish, you are greedy for preferment, that is all: and Grimscar cannot find it you since he is at odds with the Archbishop — so in consequence you come to me.

DUCHESS. God's wounds, Belladonna, will the fellow disclose or won't he?

BELLADONNA. My cousin the Duchess is as eager as I am to uncover what goes on, so tell both of us your story, sir: the bottle is at your elbow.

Odd glug glug noises as SOWSE *talks.*

SOWSE. I thank you, my lady, your grace, [although I may lack preferment, I am, with all my vices, a sincere minister of the Church of England. And whereas I despise the Puritans, when it comes to the matter of Popery, sheer horror and detestation, the Inquisition of the King of Spain — I would never have meddled with it, but my lord had such rigorous demands upon my loyalty that I -

DUCHESS. What the devil does he talk about Popery? Black Calvinism, Republicanism, is the basis of Grimscar's treason — God's blood let him tell us of that!

SOWSE. But your grace, in this exigent it is one and the same
    thing. He has been in communication — three letters have
    already passed — with the Catholic Irish, the wild O'Neill, no
    less!

DUCHESS. Blood and wounds, can this be possible!]

SOWSE. My lady, do you remember by chance at Grimscar Hall
    a particular laconical young woman —?

BELLADONNA. Madam Prudence from Geneva. I took her for
    Grimscar's trull. She'd a look in her blackamoor eye I'd seen
    somewhere in somebody's bed-chamber —

SOWSE. No, madame. She was a messenger from Ireland from
    the O'Neills and the O'Flahertys. She has since become the
    mistress of Mr Backhouse, but —

BELLADONNA. No. In no bed-chamber, and she was no woman
    neither! In straight trousers and a rug mantle, she masqueraded
    as a horse-boy from the bogs of Connacht, she talked Irish
    among Irishmen in a convent of France! You said
    O'Flaherty . . .? Of course, of course, of course . . .!

DUCHESS. Get him out of here. We've heard enough. I don't
    think he knows any more. Do you, you woundy simoniac —
    do you know any more?

SOWSE. Your grace, no indeed no, the letters she transmitted
    were in code —

DUCHESS. Hide anything from me, I'll have you pulled upon the
    rack till your leg-joints are ripped from your arse-bone! Out!

SOWSE. Your grace, my lady . . .

His feet going out, door closes on him.

DUCHESS. Belladonna, this is serious. It must be dealt with
    directly.

BELLADONNA. [It may be nothing. Hippocleides has always
    five hundred such maggots in his random inconsequent head.
    By all likelihood the O'Neills have received the whole thing
    with contempt.

DUCHESS. Oh no they have not. *Hippocleides* has received. She
    was *sent* to him. Out of Ireland.

BELLADONNA. Ah . . . I had forgot that.]

DUCHESS. There is only the one plot to be nourished out of

Ireland this season, and that is our Lord Deputy's. It is already
well-advanced. He commands the Army in Scotland and defeats
the Presbyterians. Meanwhile the King's enemies at home are
diverted by having a Parliament to talk in and talk to the
content of their chattering heart.

BELLADONNA. It is no longer only talk. They have already
passed the Bill to inhibit their dissolution —

DUCHESS. And thereby made apparent to all honest men
throughout the kingdom that they can only be got rid of by
force! So when the King's Deputy marches south with his
soldiers to coerce the rebellious Parliament —

BELLADONNA. He will be approved on all sides —

DUCHESS. By every single honest Englishman! That is, if he is
not prevented. And what d'you think can prevent him,
Belladonna, unless it were an outbreak in Ireland, his own
bailiwick, the recruiting-ground for his troops, the very genital
root of His Majesty's courage to govern? [For to tell truth, I
am afraid of the King. If he is pressed, he will give way. If he
gives way far enough, he will abandon his own Lord Deputy.
Abandon *all* of us, Belladonna; our estates will be
sequestrated: our husbands and our sons will lose their heads
upon the scaffold or be banished into the corners of the
earth!] Blood across the entrails of the Mother of God — did I
hear the poet Backhouse has taken this bitch to his bed!

BELLADONNA. I heard he had a mistress. I didn't realise it was
the same one. Do you know he has inserted her into the leading
part of his new play?

DUCHESS. Have you seen the rehearsals?

BELLADONNA. I have not. Hippocleides has determined to be
secretive. I did make him a promise I would not interfere.
They have not so much as vouchsafed me one look at the
script.

DUCHESS. I wonder why not?

BELLADONNA. Hippocleides desires to protect Backhouse from
premature criticism, and Jack Barnabas, of course, was always
particularly difficult . . .

DUCHESS. No, no that's not the reason. There is an engineer
inside this play, digging a mine of black powder underneath

our defended wall. What can we do with a mine, Belladonna,
dig a countermine, sign a contract for the work with our *own*
engineer . . .? Captain Catso.
BELLADONNA. Who?
DUCHESS. Captain Catso. A gentleman, by coincidence, of
considerable duration as a military engineer, he has been to the
German Wars, was disgraced, I believe, and came home. He has
practised many other trades. And I keep him in my house . . .

Fade down.

Scene Thirteen

Interior, very close and private.

CATSO. She keeps me, the Duchess. For various services.
As she will say, when the Duke is away
Her crude old Catso has good leave to play . . .

I am informed, gentle lady, today, I am to forage in *your*
corner. It's agreeable.
BELLADONNA. Good. You've been told? So tell *me*.
CATSO. I have served in the Army of the Austrian Emperor,
you know that. His inordinate General Wallenstein, Duke of
Friedland, demanded a triumph through the streets of the City
of Prague, he craved music, exuberant pageants, [cloth-of-gold
and bejewelled eagles, Corinthian porticoes hung with banners,
gleaming and swarming with the mottled limbs of goddesses
and the Romish saints in ecstasy. But where were the artists
and the craftsmen to be found for him, with all Bohemia a
smouldering slagheap from the worst war they had ever
experienced? So within the ranks of his own forces he looked
around for a good contriver: he was told about Catso: he sent
for me, talked to me,] and he gave me the work. For one
entire afternoon, under command of *my* pageantry, that man
became Caesar. He trampled skulls beneath his boot-heels.
And his swart head was strewn with roses. If I could do this for
Wallenstein, why not for a lord called Grimscar?

BELLADONNA. Very well. I will recommend to Mr Barnabas
that you be appointed to design and construct the moveable
scenery for the play. As soon as you are thoroughly installed
within the rehearsals, you will use your own discretion as to
exactly what happens next. It shouldn't be difficult.

CATSO. Indeed not. Two months after his great triumph in
Prague, General Wallenstein lay dead. I have an ammunition-
pouch in my quarters knows more than a little about the
bullets that killed him.

BELLADONNA. Captain, I will not have Grimscar done hurt to:
I want him my man and no-one else's, and that's it.

CATSO. Oh yes . . . I'll tell you another one. In Silesia, five years
ago, there was a debauched Rittmeister had inquiry made by
me into the character of his Colonel's wife. She was a Polack,
he desired to seduce her, he needed to know how. I was able
to tell him she was a paid spy of the King of Sweden: and the
episode concluded with the betrayal of a fortress, the
execution by firing-squad of the Colonel and three Lieutenants,
and the promotion of that Rittmeister to the Command of a
Brigade.

BELLADONNA. What happened to the Polack?

CATSO. *I* did. But that happened by the way, by pure chance . . .
If you don't want it here, we can always do it different . . .

Fade out.

Scene Fourteen

*Fade up — sounds behind a closed door of music and dancers
rehearsing — a Dancing-master going* 'One-two-one-two' *etc.*

BARNABAS. My lord, these are the invoices for Captain Catso's
decoration: twenty guineas for gold-leaf is in my opinion
appalling. I felt I must refer them to you before I approved
them.

GRIMSCAR. I place, as always, Mr Barnabas, the fullest trust in
your artistic judgement. You need not worry about your bills,

they will certainly be met, provided you can assure me they
are justified by the subsequent splendour of the production.

BARNABAS. There is no doubt about that, my lord. Captain
Catso looks and talks like a pirate from Tortuga, but God's
wounds, he knows his business. It is a delight to declaim in
front of his *periaktoi*, and his costumes are an Elysian dream.
Particularly those for the women.

GRIMSCAR. Tell me, how *are* the women?

BARNABAS. Oh much what I would have expected. High-priced
courtesans with good voices. Undeniably, they will please.
Tom Backhouse has taken care they have little to do but sing
and dance. Except for Mistress Margery — his own doxy, is she
not? Split me, but she's a queer one. She rehearses all the time
as though she were no more than one-quarter awake, and when
I speak to her she has no answer but 'yes, Mr Barnabas — no,
Mr Barnabas — whatever you think best' . . . I am considering
cutting a good deal of her part.

GRIMSCAR. Don't do that.

BARNABAS. My lord?

GRIMSCAR. She plays Esther. I have read the script. Her role I
believe is crucial.

BARNABAS. You know the title has been changed? It is now
called 'The Tragedy of Haman and his Contentious Rebellion
against the Commands of the King of Persia'. What I might
term the balancing-point of the whole play has been shifted —

GRIMSCAR. Without alteration to the text?

BARNABAS. Without alteration, so far: more a matter of the
emphasis of the production, my lord. But I believe it will
require certain loppings and prunings the better to consolidate
it. You did say, did you not — in my artistic judgement,
complete trust . . .?

GRIMSCAR. I had better not interfere. You must arrange all this
with Backhouse. By the same token I do not wish to intrude
upon your rehearsal: I have a conference at Westminster, I will
take up no more of your time —

*Knock on door. It opens, letting in rehearsal noises more
loudly.*

STAGE-MANAGER. Excuse me, my lord — Mr Barnabas,
  Captain Catso's here with one of them costumes for the King
  of Persia's concubines, he says will you look at it this minute,
  give him time before dinner to sort out your modifications,
  right?
BARNABAS. My compliments to Captain Catso, I'll see him in a
  moment. Good day to you, my lord, most grateful, I am sure . . .
GRIMSCAR. Thank you, Mr Barnabas, good day.

  GRIMSCAR's *footsteps going out.*

BARNABAS. Will you give a call for Tom Backhouse, please?
STAGE-MANAGER *(going away)*. Mr Backhouse!
BACKHOUSE *(from a distance)*. I'm here . . .

  Comes in and shuts door.

  Look here, Jack, that dancing-master has not the faintest
  notion of what to do with these damned dumbshows. I've just
  now been watching them run through the overthrow of
  Careless Carnality and Vaunting Ambition. It looks like a
  Saturday night brawl in a Fleet Street thieves' kitchen — it's
  ridiculous. These personified abstractions have got to look *real*,
  but for God's sake make sure it's the right type of reality!
  We are not dealing with pickpockets — but enormous and
  most dangerous political forces to be purged from the
  commonwealth of Persia.
BARNABAS. I wanted to talk to you about that. You see, Tom,
  for some reason you have contrived to present these episodes in
  the manner of the old bad popular theatre of — what — at least
  fifty years ago? As they are written I cannot believe any
  audience of today will be prepared to take them seriously.
  I naturally assumed there was an element of parody: and the
  dancing-master agrees with me. We worked it out between us
  last night after you'd gone to bed. Besides, if the dumbshows
  are presented as half-comical, the solemn tirades of Haman will
  be illuminated by contrast — no?
BACKHOUSE. No.
BARNABAS *(after a pause)*. Tom Backhouse you are an obstinate
  provocative son of a whore.

BACKHOUSE. No. I know my business. I wrote what I wrote and I'm expecting you to do it.

BARNABAS. And then all this jingle-jangle rim-ram-ruff of your rhymed couplets — whatever way it is spoken, it can *not* be made important!

BACKHOUSE. Yes it can. I showed you how, the very first day. If you can't do it, let me. Let me work with the actors alone and I promise you within five hours —

BARNABAS. You will have pulled out and unravelled every stitch in the goddamned knitting from top to bottom of three weeks' work! Tom, I will not permit it! I am master of this company or I am nothing, Tom: and moreover I do most apprehensively misdoubt the suitability of this play at such a critical time in the fortunes of the kingdom. Let me tell you, if this were going on in the public theatre, I am morally certain that the royal censor would object to it.

BACKHOUSE. Nonsense. Lord Grimscar has approved it, it is presented in a private house — it does not have to pass the censor. And even if it did, what could he say against the theme of it — a mighty empire delivered from the threat of Civil War, as recounted in Holy Writ? His Majesty is devout, and presumably so is his censor: the place of the performance is a house of approven loyalty. And so are the actors that perform.

BARNABAS. So we are, so we are — as every man in the profession. But this and that, you know, *has* been said about the activities of Lord Grimscar . . . Tom, these are dangerous times: we do have to look to our own proper safety: to the safety of the future of the profession — don't forget it. I want to talk to you about Esther . . . I am aware it is delicate. The young woman, your — your friend, she has withal such a tight-mouthed and discomfortable spirit — she — she —

BACKHOUSE (*ominous*). Aye? And she what?

BARNABAS (*with a nervous gulp*). If she is not capable of the full intensity of the part, then the part is too large for her and the public will fall asleep. So it must be cut.

CATSO. Camarado, I have the costume.

BARNABAS. One moment, Catso, please! On the other hand,

if she *can* play it with all the vigour it seems to call for —
then the tragic dilemma of Haman is proportionately
diminished: we are left with nothing but a crude piece of one-
sided invective in favour of the Jews — and who gives a damn
for the Jews? So the part must be cut.

BACKHOUSE. No. Both the part and the casting are *correct:* I
stand fast by them: I will *prove* them correct, by God I will
prove it in your teeth!

He slams out.

CATSO: Why, what ails our severe playwright all of a sudden,
Camarado —? Can it be he has come to realise that this his
new strange work doth betoken some diminution of his
erstwhile unquestioned genius . . .? I hear many of the actors
say so . . . do you agree with them? Myself, I am no great
critic . . . Will you tell me, Camarado, who *does* give a damn
for the Jews? There are some of them in England, so far as I
know.

BARNABAS. Of course the fanatic Puritans interminably
describe themselves as the Chosen People of God —

CATSO. Did Grimscar properly compensate you for that
disgraceful affair in Yorkshire . . .? An irregular preacher, was
there not, name of Grip, interrupted 'Julius Caesar' in Act One
Scene Two? Did you know he has been admitted to Grimscar's
lodgings here in London, by the back door, and after dark?
I mean Grimscar is a Parliament-man and Parliament is
constitutional: but when it comes beyond mere Parliament,
towards blood on the knives of the ravening mob, great
churches and grange-houses burnt to the ground, rapine and
manslaughter and mayhem — Camarado, what then? I'll tell
you one thing what then — you can tear to pieces your
rehearsal-roster, and my wings, flats and borders, three-parts
painted as they are, will be good for nothing but kindling! In
the meantime, we get on with 'em. Will you look at this
Concubine?

CATSO goes to the door, opens it and calls out:

(Calling.) Katerina, come forward, you devil, and exhibit yourself!

Bare feet treading in, with ankle-bells. Rustle of costume. Door shuts.

Oh yes . . . a few variations in the silver braid below her bosom — but what do you think of it as a basic outline?

BARNABAS *(sulkily)*. I promised Backhouse he would have approval of all the designs. We should wait until he —

CATSO. You are the commanding-officer of this company, Camarado — I want *your* opinion, *yours*, without influence or prejudice . . . Katerina, walk up and down. Put out your belly, revolve your haunches.

Ankle bells jingle. He claps his hands in time to her paces.

Ein-zwei, ein-zwei, ein-zwei . . . are the bells on her ankles too loud, do you think?

BARNABAS. I am not in the frame to attend to it now —

CATSO. Camarado, you *must!* Katerina has a rehearsal in there with the dancing-master in — in —?

KATERINA. A quarter of an hour.

CATSO. She's a great deal to tell you before she goes to it. Let her talk.

BARNABAS. Captain Catso. I don't like this.

CATSO. Let her talk. Katerina . . .? Come on, girl, last evening you were scarcely so mute in my quarters.

KATERINA. Sir, it doth strike hard that I must thus redeliver in the presence of authority the unconsidered fragments of our careless and, I thought intimate, seclusion. But inasmuch, Mr Barnabas, as this gentleman last evening took occasion before I did to dispraise Mistress Margery, and thereby induced me to give breath to my own small jealousy in the hope of his continuing favours, I said what I said and it cannot be now stopped-up: there is no doubt that the lady has —

BARNABAS. Do you bring here this plaguey malcontent to disturb the good spirit between me and my Company, Catso? God wither me, sir, do you think that I —

CATSO. No, I don't. And her small jealousy is only the spring of the cataract. Talk, you preprovident vulture, and sweep him away with it: talk!

KATERINA. Herself and her paramour Backhouse have privily

concocted an additional epilogue for the play, at all point opposed to those five trite moral couplets overtly set forward within the Company, Mr Barnabas. I have heard them, behind closed doors, rehearse it the one to the other, when they thought they were alone. I can tell you, God damn her, in such context, your Hibernian black-moor is a new woman, she performs Esther like a Fury from Hell — she hath conspired with this poet to take hold of his play and distort it to a Gorgon-mask!

BARNABAS *(after a pause)*. Captain Catso, if this be true, we have in our midst a traitor to the unparalleled heritage of our most glorious English stage, sir! Will you tell me for what reason? Will you tell me what I should do . . .?

    Fade out.

Scene Fifteen

Interior.

PEARL *(tensely)*. Tom, this is not right — I am not getting it right! We will go through it again, whether it is midnight or five hours later! End of the last act: angelic choir appears in the firmament on a painted transparency by courtesy of Captain Catso. Divine Justice in blue-and-silver descends from the heavens and speaks — give me the lines — I'll do the business.

BACKHOUSE *(flatly)*.
  'Behold the judgement now of Heaven above
  Righteous with anger, fervent with God's Love . . .'

PEARL *(during and between his lines)*. Queen Esther in her royal robes: Haman is led to the gallows: everyone else stands back to the sides of the stage. I am concealed by the moving scenery . . .

BACKHOUSE.
  'Behold the tyrant void of all his power
  Receive his doom within the very hour —

PEARL. I tear off in a twinkling my cloth-of-gold, my jewelled
    diadem —
BACKHOUSE.
    'God is not mocked: and great Kings are not blind
    To growth of evil in the greedy mind
    Of those their servants who betray their trust . . .'

    I have never in my life come up with such miserable rubbish —
    I reckon Barnabas believes it's the best speech in the whole
    play . . .
PEARL (hissing). Get on with it, Tom!
BACKHOUSE.
    'Secret conspiracy ends ever in the dust:
    And cruel collusion, howe'er so sly provoked
    Shall break in two once Justice is invoked . . .'

    Open the flats. You are discovered, you —
PEARL (panic-filled). Oh my God I won't be ready —!
BACKHOUSE. You have got to be ready! The full strength of the
    company lines up for the last exit, and Margery, you are
    discovered: all complete in your new costume, black gown,
    white starched collar, your pen in one hand, parchment scroll
    in the other!
PEARL. Oh yes, the complete country-cousin of the Reformed
    Religion — your fear-bitten bitch of a mistress, that's who,
    with an epilogue to deliver: Tom, I am terrified, this is not
    going to work! Oh why could you not have written out your
    true epilogue, let Grimscar have given it to Barnabas at the
    outset, had courage of your conviction, for God's sake, been
    bold with the man and told him!
BACKHOUSE. Told him what? That at the end of the play you
    are no longer Queen Esther dead and buried for thousands of
    years, but the very spirit and shape of the most implacable
    new-fangled enmity to the Crown and Throne of England?
PEARL. The very spirit and shape of the intention of this play!
    We have an intention to our play —
BACKHOUSE. We agreed it could not be prematurely disclosed!
PEARL. We did not! Through my ignorance of the habit of your
    damned London theatre, I allowed you to pursue your

incredible strategy to wherever you believed you could catch
up with it and hold it. The result — I am now encumbered with
rehearsing two quite different roles: the second one, the real
one, takes its whole tone from the secret epilogue. When I
perform it — if I *do* perform it, Backhouse, whatever may be
the effect on the audience, I can tell you these actors will
never forgive *you!* Oh easy enough for me to slip away again
to my own people. But you, among *your* people, from that day
you are a ruined man!

BACKHOUSE. None but yourself have put me into this peril: and
none but yourself can betray me and abandon me here. But if
I am ruined, so is Grimscar. Finish Grimscar —

PEARL. — and finish O'Neill . . .! Ah sure, it comes back to me
bolt-upright at the last, as it should, and I know it. I know too
that this play has done nothing for you but bring you home to
the place where you should always have been: whereas *me* —
out of the stark-naked slavery of the grave, I have hauled
myself forth with it into the centre of the world: I have built
myself with my own two hands my humanity for myself: and
I shall not let go of it . . .! Behind the scenery, as arranged, I
must contrive, so, to change my shape. New costume put here,
properties there: ten lines and some music to cover the
business. God I'll not even have time to button myself at the
neck — you'll have to be there, Backhouse, to help me: you
know that? (*Her voice removes as though she is walking away
down the room.*)

BACKHOUSE. I do. I'll be there. Speak the dialogue. I'll give you
the cue — '. . . Shall break in two once Justice is invoked . . .'
Carry on —

PEARL (*vioce removed: a new artificial quality in it, hard,
menacing*).
'Justice invoked indeed . . .! Sirs, hearken to its call;
Crying the Price that now must Pay For All!
This is no longer Persia: England, no place else,
Where wheat from tares, true men from false
Are now to be divided. Upon this parchment-scroll
Writ in black ink as black as their own deed:
The names of those whom you well know have tried —

And failed — to fix upon this realm the chain
Of bondage everlasting. Therefore I stride
Among you, as you see me, small and dark and plain
In feature as in dress, holding the quill
Wherewith to write against each public crime
The penalty you choose for it. Sirs, I await your will . . .'

So one after the other I read all the names aloud —

BACKHOUSE. While Grimscar and his friends in the audience
demand impeachment before Parliament, one name upon the
other, till we come to the Archbishop, and then the Lord
Deputy. And then —

PEARL. Do we dare to read out the King . . .?

BACKHOUSE. That depends upon Grimscar.

PEARL. Oh far too bloody much depends upon Grimscar. The
whole future of Ireland depends upon Grimscar. O'Neill will
do nothing till he has heard what has Grimscar done. He said
so in his letter. And what else can he do? What else can *we*
do . . .?

BACKHOUSE. We can present this goddamned play, girl, see it
through to the finish and curdle the blood with it . . .
One moment, before we continue, there is one thing to be said:
Too true, with your bereft craziness, you have well curdled *my*
thin blood
Too true, I may well in the upshot receive my ruin —
If so, I walked into it blithe and alive to all it might mean:
Pearl upon a bright new brooch shining out at my withered
throat,
Pearl like a descended star full aflame in the pit of my bed,
Pearl every word hitherto unheard of all the poetry that works
in my head —
Flood-tide in the wide sea:
It is you that have made it, not me . . .

Bravo bravissimo, nunc haberunt terrorem —! Let's go
through the whole thing from the beginning of the last act . . .

   Fade down.

Scene Sixteen

Interior. Very close and private.

GRIP *(in a whisper)*. I have told you before and I tell you again, Grimscar — no! This is not sufficient! Impeachment before Parliament, [constitutional procrastination,] against a man like the King's Lord Deputy with his army at his back, this counsel will be confounded, as it was confounded before, [as the counsel of Ahithophel was confounded by Hushai the Archite. The generation of Abel can only withstand Cain by seizing the weapons of Cain —

GRIMSCAR *(also whispering)*. The sword of the Lord and of Gideon . . .? No.] Mr Grip, Civil War will betoken naught but the complete failure of our politics, Mr Grip: the way you talk one would think it were a long-looked-for consummation! And moreover we have no soldiers. They can only be levied by Parliament as the result of a correct process in response to a precise defiance, by the King, against the law, and the people, and the constitution of the realm. If his Deputy is impeached, very like such defiance will indeed be forthcoming — but until then —

GRIP. Until then the Lord Deputy is in command of his army in Scotland: he can defy you whenever he wants. While he is where he is, it is useless to impeach him, unless first you take control with the power of the godly of the royal arsenals and storehouses in all other parts of the kingdom —

GRIMSCAR. Mr Grip, this is frenzy distemper —

GRIP. It is already prepared for: upon the signal in one day it can be accomplished, Grimscar. We want to know what will be that signal. Parliamentary debate gives the enemy too much forewarning. We require summat else, short, sharp, catastrophic, like a handclap from the angel of God.

GRIMSCAR. I have told you, I think, about Mr Backhouse and his new play?

GRIP. [And I have told you what *I* think about stage-plays . . . *(Pause.)* Nonetheless,] if you can prove such profanity can indeed be set to work in the cause of righteousness, we are prepared to regard you as a justified instrument in the hand of God. If [that proof is] not [given, if London and all England are not immediately made aware that through this stage-play the gentlemen of Westminster have declared their whole-heartedness in the fulfilment of our liberty, then we look for another sign:] we travel our *own* road [regardless. For] our word is the word of the Common People of England, made most powerful in the strength of the Lord [— not a gentleman, not a nobleman, can determine the course of our progress.] Grimscar, we will wait and watch.

Fade down.

Scene Seventeen

Voices murmuring and chattering in a large hall. Music plays a light overture, at a distance.

BELLADONNA *(to herself).* The more we were forewarned of these treacherous ill-purposes, the more it seemed expedient that this play should not take place.

DUCHESS *(to herself).* My cousin Belladonna is a woman of weak stomach. She should know we have a plan, it cannot now be amended. Until the upshot we must contain ourselves: let her glorious broad hall be filled with whomever comes in.

BELLADONNA *(to herself).* My friends, who are the King's friends, and all the damned black Puritan cockroaches unwontedly seduced hither by the warlock enchantment of Grimscar . . .

DUCHESS. Will you look at them as they stand in the corner? Never in all their lives have they been to a play before. God, but to see the nostrils of these austere sons of Israel quiver at the sweet reek of the smoke from the altars of Rimmon.

BELLADONNA. Ssh . . . we are pledged to give them no words but gratulation . . . *(To herself.)* Food and wine being passed among them, over two hundred candles set flaring above their heads, they take their places for the music to begin to resound —

*The overture has finished, there is a pause, and then a new
loud blast of music.*

GRIMSCAR. There was high music, there was a silence: and then
the curtains were withdrawn. Behold how Captain Catso had
prepared for us all a Paradise!

BELLADONNA. The King of Persia and all his Satraps, attired
like Paladins in green and gold . . .

ACTOR (*playing Ahasuerus; at a distance*).
'I am Ahasuerus Emperor
King of the World from Egypt to the bounds
of Himalaya and the Indian Sea —
I myself made not my great estate
But those who came before me, with their sword,
Their host of horsemen and the royal courage
Of their right hand. They left me everything
And only by my wisdom shall I keep it . . .'

Fade out.

Fade in — play continuing.

BARNABAS (*playing Haman; at a distance*).
'Who is this Mordecai who bows not down to me?
Within the King's great gate he sits and stares
Defiance as I pass: does he not know
I am the Great King's Minister: I am myself
The wisdom of the King appointed here
To rule his head, and contradict his heart
If ever it become a human heart
Instead of royal? Go bring that man to me
And let me see if I can fathom him . . .'

GRIMSCAR *has begun to speak over* BARNABAS' *speech.*

GRIMSCAR. There was no doubt in my mind as I listened to his
verses that Backhouse at last was proven a tragic poet of no less
quality than the very greatest of the generations dead and gone.
I looked over towards him to rejoice with him there-for: good
God he was shaking with rage!

Fade down BARNABAS *and* GRIMSCAR *together.*

Sound of the play's dialogue behind these speeches, but distorted so that the precise words are not always clearly heard.

ACTOR (*playing Ahasuerus; his first two-and-a-half lines clearly heard*).
'Invoke the ancient statute, none shall walk
Unheralded in presence of the King
On pain of death . . . unless the King hold out
His golden sceptre as a gracious token
That he himself in mercy shall abate
The sometime rigour of the Persian law.'

PEARL (*playing Esther*).
'It is the Queen, your love, that standeth here
Braving alone the fury of that law . . .'

ACTOR (*playing 1st Courtier*).
'My lord, the statutes of the Medes and Persians
Must not abate for *female* mutiny!'

ACTOR (*playing 2nd Courtier*).
'Of all your subjects it is meet your love
Should prove the most obedient, my lord,
You must not pardon her, she is unnatural!'

BACKHOUSE. From the very start I apprehended we were most treacherously undone. Crucial speeches for no reason disappeared from the text; insidious new harmony applied to the music turned passion and terror into petulant pathos: the costumes, the scenery were all sprinkled with tag-rag fal-de-lals that were most certainly never evident upon the sketches I had approved. Nonetheless my brave Margery was performing her role as though the ghost of my old master Ben Jonson stood behind her ten feet tall . . .

PEARL (*playing Esther. Suddenly clear of the distortion.*)
'Here I am and bolt-upright before Persia and all the world:
If I perish I will perish: but my word will have been heard . . .!'

Her voice is suddenly muffled, distorted again, and is covered with music.

BACKHOUSE. And yet every time she gave utterance there was a movement upon the stage, a creaking and groaning of machinery, scenery, curtains or a burst of music — and a whole chorus of bare-breasted women into every episode where they were not wanted!

GRIMSCAR. Yet for all this there were the words of my poet and they *were* heard. I saw Puritans of a sudden discover themselves delighted, Cavaliers cut short in their approbation of the dancing women —

PEARL *(playing Esther; heard clearly again)*.
'No King who gives his heart and hand and brain
Into the belly of his Minister should ever dare wear Crown
Unbludgeoned by the vengeance of his people —!'

Stormy applause and booing.

GRIMSCAR. And so it went on, till we came to the last act and the last scene of the last act . . .

Fade down.

Music and sounds of stage-machinery.

PEARL. With a discordance of those damnable pulleys and blocks, Divine Justice comes down into the midst of this mortal world —

ACTOR *(playing Diving Justice)*.
'Behold the judgement now of Heaven above
Righteous with anger, fervent with God's Love . . .'

His speech from Scene 15 continues, interspersed (and prolonged by musical effects) throughout the next section of dialogue.

PEARL. The flats close . . .

Voice of Divine Justice becomes indistinct.

I am behind them, my new costume laid out to my hand —
Backhouse beside me stands ready to help me to change —

BACKHOUSE. In the darkness and the heat and all that dust at the rear of the stage, I was never certain to the day of my death exactly what did happen . . .

PEARL. It was Catso like a black tiger out of the darkness upon Tom's back —

BACKHOUSE. And his dagger went into my body —

CATSO. *Ein — zwei — drei — und schlag-ihn-todt!*

BACKHOUSE. Three times against my rib bones and down into the liver: I fell to the floor: my mouth choked with a vomit of blood —

PEARL. All in the dark and so quick I was not even able to scream. I was held by the wrist. I was dragged forward. Divine Justice concluding his speech . . .

ACTOR *(playing Divine Justice).*
  '. . . And cruel collusion, howe'er so sly provoked
  Shall break in two once Justice is invoked!'

  The scenery opens allowing Divine Justice's last words to be suddenly heard loud and clear. Music triumphant.

CATSO. Lady, the scene is open. Shall we walk before the public and deliver to them your epilogue . . .

GRIMSCAR *(against a background of astonished gasps and cries etc.).* He was dressed as the lowest type of grotesque priapic clown, on his head he wore the mask of a goggle-eyed demon, he had Pearl's right arm twisted cruelly behind her shoulder-blades, he had caught her, God in Heaven, at the very middle of her costume change, her garments fell down around her loins, she was totally and shamefully exposed in the glare of the candles. Her mouth was wide open with shock, and it looked as though she laughed at us, as though on fire with blasphemous mockery.

  The music has wavered and is now silent. The audience has also fallen silent. CATSO speaks in the echoing hall.

CATSO.
  Justice invoked — my lords, what can we say?
  Justice, like Truth, buttock-naked here today
  Has come to dance for you, and play!
  God's Word, King's Rule, Parliamentary fuss-and-trouble,
  In the shuddering of this mortal flesh are worth no more a bubble—!

Music begnis again, jerky.

CATSO. Dance, Margery, dance, Pearl — dance, my crop-haired
    queen!

GRIMSCAR. Before us all he was leaping like a wild animal in the
    heat of lust, and he jerked at her, compelling her to appear to
    leap likewise . . .

CATSO. Queen of the world, my lords, doth she not now
    maintain Her state triumphant on your every inward thought —?

> *A crash of a falling body: a scream from* PEARL; *a yell
> from* CATSO 'Hurroo . . .!', *and the music stops in mid-beat.*

GRIMSCAR. We saw her flung like a rag of wet linen to one side
    of the stage. The curtains closed upon both of them: and
    incontinent his devil's head came back through the gap in the
    curtain —

CATSO.
    And yet what was she but the naked slave
    To the poor heart-root of one half-finished poet?
    Oh yes he made his play and at the end
    Had nothing left for you to comprehend
    But that which you have seen:
    Your own stark lustful flesh, my lords,
    Will inform you what we mean . . .
    Oh yes . . .

> *A moment of silence, then outcry.*

GRIMSCAR. For the Roundheads in that audience the blasphemy
    was absolute. Whatever I said to them I could never persuade
    them now that Tom Backhouse and myself had nothing to do
    with this abomination of desolation. My position within
    their party was for good and all discredited. Not even the
    messenger gasping and covered with mud, who burst into the
    hall at that moment, could make any difference. He cried out
    to the company —

MESSENGER. The King's Army has been defeated by the Scotch
    Presbyterians!

Sudden silence again.

The whole country is now aware that the Lord Deputy has failed in his trust!

Explosion of excited hubbub, feet stumbling over benches to get out of the hall.

DUCHESS. If the Lord Deputy is unable to protect the King against his subjects, then how can the King protect the Lord Deputy? Belladonna, finish this, finish it now — every person of the King's faction must look now to their own proper safety —!

Distant sounds as of people running up and down stairs and along passages in another part of the building, calling unintelligibly. Otherwise silence.

BELLADONNA. I went round behind the stage. Captain Catso had heard the messenger: he was dumbfounded: and the woman had not yet been killed.

Moaning.

BELLADONNA. He had her held bound and gagged in a small dark closet upstairs: there was a short bone-handled knife hanging from a cord round her neck. I took hold of it.

PEARL. She drove the point deep into both of my eyes. And she split my top lip to the division of my nostrils. She cut notches into my cheeks and my ears. After that, they wrapped rags round me: they kicked me out at a back door . . .

Scene Eighteen

Rising wind heard, mingled with faint music as from PEARL's *dream (Scene Eleven) gradually increasing in volume through the ensuing speech.*

PEARL. After that: the King's Lord Deputy, by Act of Parliament, was impeached, and his head was taken off. His friend the Archbishop was also impeached, and his head was

taken. Civil War came upon England. The King's head was
taken off. Civil War came upon Ireland. O'Neill now
understood there was not one party in England any good to
him any more, and he raised his rebellion as originally
intended. He was misleadingly accused of unprecedented
bloodshed. As a result, the whole of Ireland laid waste,
[oh most barbarous,] by the revolutionary army of Oliver
Cromwell. Gideon Grip had been made a Quartermaster-
Serjeant in that army, but he was hanged at his General's
order for democratic agitation. [Captain Catso, who at first
had been fighting for the King, transferred his allegiance, and
went to Ireland with the Cromwellians. He was promoted full
Colonel, and rewarded by a grant of land, two thousand acres
in the County Cork. Lord Grimscar lost all his friends and fled
to Holland to avoid his creditors. Belladonna lost all her
fortune because of the war, she fled to France and died of the
pox.] Tom Backhouse whom I had loved, never recovered of
his wounds, and never wrote another play.

   Music ceases, wind noises continue.

Every theatre throughout the land was closed down by Act of
Parliament: and from that day to this the word of the Common
People of England, most powerful in the strength of the Lord,
had little or nothing to do with the word of their tragic poets
or the high genius of their actors. You might say this did small
hurt to the body and bones, but deeper, within the soul . . .
Let them live with it.
    As for myself, made ugly and made blind,
    I had to live the best way I could find.
(*She chants.*)
'For the mercy of Christ give a penny to the poor blind
    woman . . .'
My final change of shape, you may believe,
Did not assist me long time to survive.
(*Chants again.*)
For the mercy of Christ, my masters, give a penny to the poor
    blind woman . . .'

   The tapping of her stick recedes: the wind blows.
   Fade down.

Appendix A

The passage between brackets in Scene Five, as marked with an asterisk, was replaced in the BBC production by the following:

PEARL. The northern province. Where the King's Protestants, English and Scots, have been planted in the lands taken by force from the Catholic people. There is an exiled Catholic chief, O'Neill of the Clan O'Neill: and he is the man who has had me sent here. He says, every dispossessed Catholic clan in the north is about to rise up. And not only the north — my own people, the O'Flahertys from Connemara in the west, and many more. It has been said, a day cometh, a great reckoning. The people of God will destroy in their thousands the people of God. The Lady Eire, it has been said, will walk barefoot on the mountains in her mantle of bright green.

> They have convinced themselves beyond denial
> Starvation breasts at once will be made full
> Only because distracted brave O'Neill
> Sees nothing else to do but kill
> And kill and kill and kill and kill . . .

I ask you, through whose fault we have been driven to it, whose is the fault?

GRIMSCAR. There is no need to weep at it, it is too soon, we discuss politics, we explore technique . .

BACKHOUSE. If we are passionate, there will be errors made. Lady, there will be errors, we over-run ourselves, we will all fall down!

PEARL *(controlling her rage)*. We will not. We explore technique. My lord has said so: it is quite true. My people, you see, have heard that you, though a great lord, from the upper house of the dissolved Parliament, have attempted to make alliance with the Scots Presbyterians and the persecuted extreme Puritans in this country. So very good. O'Neill desires you should extend that alliance to *his* people. Will you do it?

BACKHOUSE. Wait on, now wait a minute: now let's get this clear. They have sent you into England to ask disaffected English Protestants to take up the cause of the Catholics in Ireland?

GRIMSCAR. No, it won't do. The Irish Catholics are determined
   upon massacre, you have said so — the murder and massacre of
   hundreds and hundreds of Protestants —

PEARL. Hippocleides, third Marquess Grimscar, if we are
   passionate, there will be errors made. O'Neill is no more of a
   barbarian than you are. He will massacre nobody — unless the
   Protestants of Ireland are so foolish as to help the King's Lord
   Deputy maintain his tyrannical control: which control is
   excused to them in these terms — if they do *not* help him,
   then the King of Spain will invade Ireland.

GRIMSCAR. And will he?

PEARL. He will not of course. O'Neill knows there will be no help
   from the King of Spain. But on the other hand — the
   Scotsmen, the Presbyterians, whom the Lord Deputy will
   attack, are the brothers of the Irish Protestants. And O'Neill
   would make them *his* brothers. He says, how far is *religion* the
   root cause of all this broil? Surely, he says, it is land, and
   outrageous taxation, and the right to self-government, and
   land again, land, which has been stolen from *all* the people.
   But if O'Neill and his people go to war without friends, then
   destruction upon Ireland for evermore and no remedy . . .

BACKHOUSE. My lord, will you write to O'Neill? Put it clear to
   him: politics. Resolution of the religious differences can be
   left on one side for a matter of years if need be —

PEARL. Will you write to him?

GRIMSCAR. Commit my treason to pen-and-ink? Are you mad?

PEARL. Let you dictate a letter: I will put it into Irish and then
   reverse it into an agreed cipher. He will reply in the same
   manner. I am instructed to remain here and interpret the reply
   when it comes. Among your household in these garments I will
   not be conspicuous.

BACKHOUSE. Lady, in these garments, why, you are the
   country-cousin of the Reformed Religion! No difficulty I
   suppose about conveyance of the letter?

GRIMSCAR. Dr Sowse will arrange something.

BACKHOUSE. I mistrust Dr Sowse.

GRIMSCAR. Tom, you and I will discuss this letter. *(As he moves
   to the door.)* We will leave the lady here, Tom, if she does not

object to the unseemly state of your bedroom.

> BACKHOUSE *laughs.*
> *They go out and the door shuts.*

Scene Six

PEARL (*to herself, after a pause*). They keep me waiting till near
midnight . . .

Appendix B

The passage between brackets in Scene Nine, as marked with an
asterisk, was replaced in the BBC production by the following:

PEARL. He offers to restore the complete proper sovereignty of
the Four Provinces of Ireland into the hands of the Irish
themselves . . . complete . . . really complete . . .?

BACKHOUSE. In return, as it says, for O'Neill's guarantee that
he will not attack the King's Protestants in their northern
settlement, but instead will devote his forces to the defence of
the English Parliament against the tyranny of the Crown: if
O'Neill will give us that, I think Parliament will refuse him
nothing.

PEARL. Not even the toleration throughout Ireland of the
Catholic Church . . .? My father in the new-found land had a
bag of medicine, as he called it. Without that bag he would
have been no chief: but an outcast and a mark for every stone
and arrow in the forest. Would you say that your English King,
as head of your English Church, possessed his *own* bag of some
such art-magic? Take it away from him — you'd have . . . what?

BACKHOUSE. By the Lord . . . a Republic . . . a free Republic of
the English Commonwealth. Ah God, if we must come to it,
then come to it we must! And yet, and yet, while we are in

the process of making it — Tom Backhouse must sit down and construct an orgiastical new play — for Belladonna no less! They want nymphs in it with round bare legs, Bacchanalians, a pair of lovers who turn out to be brother and sister, and at the end a bloody great rainbow and Diana coming down in a cloud. By God if anyone's to come down in a cloud, what's the matter with — Gideon Grip! For without such as him to cheer out their throats for me, I find nowt any more in the whole of this England fit for the tip of my pen. We spoke once to the whole people. But these day we have rejected the homespun jackets, the square-toed shoes, and the forthright word of the godly tradesmen. And by God they've rejected *us*. There are those in the Parliament have said openly they'd close down every playhouse if they once attained full power. And I *want* them to attain full power. And the whole of my life's work will be broken in two by it . . .

PEARL. Or else altogether made new: as new as a new Republic?

BACKHOUSE. Pearl, Margery, whatever your name is, housekeeper, mistress, whatever your status: I am not a young man. Where am I to go, child, what am I to do . . .?

PEARL. This book . . . of the Scripture . . . Gideon Grip holds in his fist. What does it contain?